Living with

For my mother

Living with Teenagers

Martin Herbert

Basil Blackwell

British Library Cataloguing in Publication Data

Herbert, Martin
  Living with teenagers.
  1. Adolescence
  I. Title
  305.2'35   HQ796
  ISBN 0–631–15298–9

Library of Congress Cataloging in Publication Data

Herbert, Martin.
  Living with teenagers.
  Bibliography: p.
  Includes index.
  1. Adolescence.   2. Adolescent psychology.
  I. Title.
  HQ796.H398   1987   305.2'35   86–28313
  ISBN 0–631–15298–9 (pbk.)

Typeset in 11 on 12½pt Sabon by Cambrian Typesetters,
Frimley, Surrey
Printed in Great Britain by Billing & Sons Ltd, Worcester

Contents

Contents

Preface

Many parents await their children's teenage years with a sense of gloomy foreboding. Adolescence is viewed as a phase of development to be endured rather than enjoyed, to be confronted rather than shared. So I shall address the anxieties of such parents, by providing helpful and reassuring factual information based upon many scientific studies of adolescence. I hope to allay their worst and, usually, unnecessary fears.

The theme of this book is that adolescence, if approached in the right frame of mind, can be a period of harmonious relationships or, at least, as harmonious as any other stage of development your children pass through. It would be a pity not to enjoy the years before your child leaves home. Of course, the trouble is that there are so many myths and 'disaster stories' about the 'terrible' teens. And, sadly, if you do expect the worst you are quite likely to get it. Much of adolescence's bad reputation with parents and teachers is due to self-inflicted, self-injurious and self-fulfilling prophecies.

This is not to say that adolescence does not have its share of problems, as does every other stage of development. Some are unique – reactions to the new demands of physical maturity, and the challenge to be 'grown up'. Others are continuations of earlier difficulties. Whichever category it may be, parents wish to demonstrate understanding and concern.

But even concern and understanding can be too much of a good thing. A reminiscence in adulthood, by Ruth Ling, includes the comment: 'My great problem in being a teenager was that my parents, instead of allowing me to exercise my birthright to rebel against them, seemed hellbent on siding with me against authority.' One cannot win, or so it would seem from this wry, but not altogether untypical commentary on the ambivalence of adolescents on the subject of parents. They are either too understanding or not understanding enough. They set limits and are called authoritarian; they don't set limits and are thought of as permissive or uncaring. How can you help your teenager when help is resented? How do you guide when guidance is brushed aside? And how can you communicate when questions and comments are perceived as interference?

Fortunately, wise parents have no wish to win, in the sense of emerging as victors of battles and confrontations with their offspring. Rather they wish to *win through*, in the task of supporting them in their journey through adolescence to maturity.

Troubled and troublesome is the way that many of us think of teenagers. Is there any truth in this stereotype? Parents and teachers are most inclined to worry about youngsters when their actions persist in being

1 not understandable – that is, when their moods, attitudes or behaviours defy good sense and lack reason or meaning;
2 unpredictable, such that there is a Jekyll-and-Hyde-like quality of changeability, disconcerting switches in mood, friendliness and co-operation;
3 rebellious and uncontrollable, in the sense that adults are unable to impose their authority and/or the teenager seems unwilling or unable to control his or her own behaviour.

Few parents (or teachers) have not observed such forms of behaviour in a particular adolescent, at one time or another, and they tend to be resigned about such manifestations: 'Well, that's what you'd expect, isn't it, of a teenager.' It is when such actions are frequent and intense that real concern is felt; in other words, it is a matter of degree. Bearing that in mind, we can take comfort from the fact that adolescence is not invariably a time of emotional disturbance. Far from it.

Francis Bacon wrote in the sixteenth century that 'knowledge itself is power' and, today, clinical psychologists affirm that accurate self-knowledge and information about situations are therapeutically potent. Undoubtedly you can help your teenage son or daughter by your understanding of adolescence and its special features. Empathic understanding and insight are not enough; parents (and teachers) also need a supply of practical and effective strategies to apply directly to problematic circumstances as they arise.

To this end, I describe the salient features of adolescence in chapter 1, providing answers to some of the perennial questions young people ask about their changing bodies and their worries about their self-image.

Teenagers are individuals, and they are as different one from the other in their personal qualities as are children and adults. Their tendency to conform to teenage culture and fashion – some with deliberately high visibility – may present a superficial similarity which the media find convenient to exploit and headline, especially when there is a sensational incident involving young people. In this book, readers are encouraged to recognize and accept the new challenges, tasks and needs which preoccupy these sometimes 'strange' young adults who are emerging from childhood.

Chapter 1 begins by taking a look at what we mean by 'adolescence'. Chapter 2 discusses the adolescent's attempts to strike out for his or her independence, explores the relationships between young people, their parents and their peers, and looks for the elusive 'generation gap'. Chapter 3 provides information about common developmental depressions and anxieties as well as the more serious phobias (school refusal and anorexia nervosa), and chapter 4 deals with the problems of antisocial behaviour.

In chapters 5, 6 and 7, I explore some of the issues that preoccupy teenagers (and their parents): chapter 5 examines that perennial source of curiosity, excitement and disquiet, the young person's emergent sexuality; and chapters 6 and 7 deal with work and unemployment, and experimentation with alcohol and drugs.

Chapter 8 takes matters of particular concern to teachers and (no less) parents – success and failure at school, truancy, discipline and disruption in the classroom – and lists some reasons and remedies for them.

Finally, chapters 9 and 10 provide several suggestions about practical ways of helping yourself and your teenager when the going is rough.

As with my book *Caring for your Children: a practical guide*, to which this volume is a sequel, I have tried to cater not only for parents and teachers, but also for those professional groups – doctors, social workers, psychologists and probation officers – who work with adolescents and their families.

I offer the same caveat as I did for my previous guide. It is not possible, or desirable, to *prescribe* set solutions for teenage problems; each youngster, every parent and all families are unique – and so are their dilemmas. So one cannot proffer *generalized* advice to meet all cases and contingencies. What may be helpful is to have guidelines which allow you to pre-empt fraught situations by planning broad strategies of care and discipline. This is surely preferable to trailing helplessly after events.

Chapter One

The nature of adolescence

Lousy stinking school on Thursday. I tried my old uniform on, but I have outgrown it so badly that my father is being forced to buy me a new one tomorrow.

He is going up the wall but I can't help it if my body is in a growth period can I? I am only five centimetres shorter than Pandora now. My thing remains static at twelve centimetres.

(Sue Townsend, *The Secret Diary of Adrian Mole aged 13¾*)

Young Adrian Mole, tormented 'offspring' of the creative imagination of author Sue Townsend, displays in this fragment from his diary at least six common adolescent preoccupations: bodily changes, sex, school, relationships with parents and, not least, himself and the opposite sex. But is he typical? More important, what, precisely, is adolescence? It is a term so readily bandied about that you might assume that it is susceptible to a quick and precise definition. Answers are, however, not all that easy to come by; so many myths and prejudices have attached themselves to the concept of adolescence.

The notions of childhood and adulthood are clear enough. Children are wholly dependent upon their parents for love, nurturance and guidance; adults are required to be independent and able to care for themselves. Somewhere between the immaturity of childhood and the hoped-for maturity of adulthood lie the six or seven years we refer to as adolescence. That there is (and is bound to be) a stage of transition from 'irresponsibility' to 'responsibility' has been accepted from at least the time of Aristotle.

If we think of life as a journey with its own signposts and timetables, then it must be admitted that this part of the expedition is the one most poorly marked out and programmed. In our industrial and urbanized societies there are very few rituals which the community as a whole recognizes as special milestones for the various phases in a child's development. This is in contrast to preliterate societies in which formal initiation ceremonies demonstrate to children and their community that they have entered (socially and physically) the territory of adulthood.

There is no one ritual that provides children with a clear sign that they have left infancy behind. Initiation into adulthood is made up of a variety of little events which, cumulatively, *imply* that childhood is over. So, unfortunately, parents and children (or young adults) may disagree about what stage has been reached and, consequently, what rights, privileges and responsibilities are now appropriate. Confusion reigns and, where there is confusion, confrontation is likely to follow.

What is adolescence?

There is a temptation to think of teenagers as if they are members of a different species, emphasizing the strangeness, the discontinuities (rather than the many significant continuities) between children and adolescents and, indeed, adolescents and adults. The concentration on such differences can lead to stereotyping and over-generalizing in our thinking about what, after all, is a somewhat arbitrary stage of development.

While writing this book I was invited to a school concert. The young people at this 'middle' high school ranged in age from 11 to 14, and there they stood – 50 of them in a massed choir – singing for all they were worth. It was like a speeded-up image of the entire range of adolescence. A few of the youngsters were well-developed, poised young men and women. Many were awkward, unfinished-looking 'in-betweens' with rather gangly arms and legs. The others were still obviously children, and yet not altogether childlike. It was a salutary reminder to me of the rapidity of change which adolescence brings about and the potential of such change to be accompanied by unease and distress by adolescent and parents alike.

Some theorists reject the notion of adolescence as a distinct stage of development. They repudiate the idea that at puberty every child takes on a different personality. Rather the child grows by imperceptible degrees into a teenager, and the adolescent turns by degrees into an adult.

Others disagree. The confusion over the boundaries defining adolescence is revealed by the metaphors applied to it: the 'in-between stage', and 'that no-man's land between childhood and adolescence'. It has also been referred to as a 'tunnel' into which young people disappear, displaying certain kinds of character. They are then 'lost to sight' for a few years. According to this metaphor you never know what is going to emerge at the other end.

What a daunting prospect for parents and teachers (if true) when they've put so much time and effort, not to mention love and affection, into preparing the children in their care for happy and productive adulthood. Is it really such a lottery? Be reassured, adolescence *is* a distinctive phase of development because of dramatic changes in growth, and new developments in the teenager's intellectual capacities and sexuality. But it is not ephemeral or discontinuous. There are many continuities in development between what has happened in the past and what lies ahead. To a marked extent, adolescence is merely a route linking childhood with adult life, and, despite the odd detour and cul-de-sac, most youngsters turn out in recognizable form.

Let us begin by saying what adolescence is *not*. It is not a universal phenomenon; indeed, it is not very old as a period considered worthy of serious study, literary or scientific. This is presumably because adolescence, as we think of it, was not perceived to be different or separate from the rest of development. You are likely to have read that adolescence is heralded by the physical changes of puberty. True, but adolescence cannot be equated with puberty. Puberty is biologically inevitable, whereas adolescence is, in a sense, a creation of our industrial (Westernized) cultures. Adolescence had to be 'invented' (among other reasons) because of our postponement of that point in the life-span at which the child assumes adult status and responsibility. Children in preliterate societies are regarded as adults, and treated as such, when they reach puberty, at whatever age that might be.

The term 'adolescence' refers, in essence, to the *psychological* developments which are related (loosely) to the physical growth processes defined by the term 'puberty'. To put it another way, adolescence begins in biology and ends in culture – at that juncture where the boy and girl have attained a reasonable degree of psychological independence from their parents. That is why there is a lack of precision in the definition and timetabling of adolescence. There is no clear endpoint. Even the beginning point – puberty itself – is a 'movable feast', varying according to climatic and hereditary factors, and subject to being triggered or delayed by many external influences.

To the layperson, adolescence simply refers to the process of growing up – the period of transition between childhood and adulthood. It coincides roughly with the so-called 'teens', but the number of years devoted to adolescent development varies from culture to culture. In the past half-century or so, within Western societies, adolescence has become a progressively longer span of years. This reflects the mixed feelings we have about the decision as to when, in law or social custom, a young person is grown-up and responsible: old enough to drink in a pub or bar, mature enough to manage a bank account, to indulge in sexual intercourse, to get married, to fight for one's country, to vote, or to be held responsible for a criminal act.

The major task of the adolescent stage – according to many contemporary psychologists – is the individual's need to shape and consolidate his or her own identity as a unique and mature person. The development of self-identity refers to the core of an individual's character or personality and is thought to be a vital precursor to true intimacy and depth in personal relationships. It begins with adolescents' intense concern for discovering their individual nature, and ends when they have established a coherent sense of self and personal identity. This task (of *becoming* a unique person) is usually completed (to the extent that we can ever say such complex developments are resolved) between the ages of 18 and 22.

At the very foundation of adolescent self-awareness – the self image – is a representation of their body, what it is like, and how it looks to others. If there is any one event which makes adolescence stand out from the rest of childhood, it is the radical nature of the growth which occurs at the time. These physical, physiological and mental changes transform children into adults.

The changes of puberty

Many of the significant psychological changes appear to be related to the teenager's physical maturing. For example, puberty may bring about a certain self-centredness in your child. The very ground on which the young person has been standing so securely up to now begins to shift. The body your child has taken for granted becomes the focus of attention; so much is happening! Not surprisingly, there is a lot of mirror-gazing and minute scrutiny of blemishes and 'good points'.

Try not to show too much concern when your children become egocentric and self-absorbed. The many physical upheavals encountered during puberty require a focusing in on themselves while they adapt to change and come to terms with their new (or modified) body-image. It is like the canoeist who has paddled along in serene waters, able to attend to all manner of things and people around her, suddenly finding herself swirling about in the white waters of the rapids. All her concentration and energies are needed to keep the canoe upright and to maintain some reasonably safe direction. Her self-absorption at such a time would seem eminently reasonable.

The physical and physiological changes that take place (on

average) at 12 in girls, and 14 in boys, are due to the action of hormones, and are quite dramatic. Growth in virtually all parts of the body is sharply accelerated. It tends to be most rapid at the periphery and to move in toward the trunk, so the young adolescent appears to be 'all hands and feet'. Of course, size eventually gets back into proportion. During one of your son's periods of inertia or lassitude, you may be tempted to diagnose (incorrectly, it should be said) that 'he's outgrown his strength'.

All of these events are referred to as the adolescent *growth spurt*. Because the peak in growth rate occurs at different times for different parts of the body, the basic balance of the body is temporarily disturbed – producing, for some, a disconcerting sense of disequilibrium.

The end of childhood, for the boy, is signposted by an increase in the size of testes, scrotum and penis; in the girl there is an increase in the growth rates of breasts, ovaries and uterus (womb). For both sexes there is an increase in size of shoulders and hips, arms and legs, height and total body weight. Boys undergo a significant increase in their muscle tissue and strength, whereas girls develop more fatty tissue, producing their softer and more rounded contours. There is a marked increase in shoulder breadth in boys and hip width in girls.

Girls' development is two years ahead of boys', as it tends to be throughout the developmental timetable. Don't be alarmed if your child is somewhat early or late. Children vary quite markedly – the gap may be four years or more – in the age at which they become pubertal. For girls, the age at which the menstrual cycle makes its first appearance can differ by several years. One may find an early-developed girl at the age of 12 or 13 who is already physically a woman, with fully developed sexual characteristics and destined to grow very little more in height. At about the same age, and therefore in the same classroom and social group, may be a later-developing girl who is just about to begin her growth spurt and who is little more than a child in her physical characteristics. The same conspicuous differences might be seen in boys of 14 or 15. Think also of an 'early developer' at the age of 16 and a 'late developer' at the age of 13 and you can see how nonsensical it is to generalize too much about *teenagers* or *the* teenager. One is a mature-looking and possibly quite sophisticated young adult; the other is a pre-pubescent child in many ways.

Your daugther may be concerned about becoming impossibly tall – outstripping her peers even further at adolescence – because she is already tall before the event. However, girls who are already tall as pre-adolescents tend to reach the adolescent growth spurt earlier than other girls. Once your dismayed daughter and her later-maturing peers have passed the period of rapid adolescent growth their *height relationships* are more likely to return to those of pre-adolescence. Thus her worst fears of being a 'giant' among midgets are unlikely to materialize. Similarly, your son (if he is short) may view the picture above in reverse – a midget among the giants. Short boys may appear to be losing ground as a result of delays in the adolescent growth spurt, only to return later to an approximation of their initial height relationships with their fellows.

It is especially important that you show understanding at this unsettling time; since teenagers may have more social awareness now than they had before, the feeling of being out of synchrony can be intolerable at times. Adolescents are very much the victims of biological forces they cannot always comprehend. The sense of events being out of one's control is never pleasant.

Puberty is not just a matter of changes in the size and shape of the body. Physiological developments in glandular secretion, particularly those affecting sexual function, occur. Up until puberty, males and females have similar quantities of *both* sex hormones in the bloodstream, with only a slightly greater proportion of the sex-relevant hormone. Thus boys have nearly as much oestrogen (the female sex hormone) as androgen. At puberty, however, there is a sharp increase in the secretion of the sex-related hormone.

The pituitary gland at the base of the brain starts to

produce two hormones – the gonadotrophic hormones – which it releases into the bloodstream. These complex chemical substances are actually the same in both sexes, but in boys they are produced together continuously, whereas in girls they are produced one after the other in accordance with the monthly menstrual cycle.

The two hormones are the follicle-stimulating hormone (FSH) and the luteinizing hormone (LH). In boys, the FSH 'instructs' the testes to start making sperm cells, and the LH (also called the interstitial-cell-stimulating hormone) causes the testes to start making testosterone, the male sex hormone. Both the pituitary hormones cause the testes to grow, but it is testosterone that produces the other changes of puberty. These include the growth of the penis, and the deepening of the voice owing to the enlargement of the larynx. Boys' voices break, at times shifting alarmingly from low basso to high contralto. Boys also develop hair on the face, body and limbs. The same hormone causes loss of hair on the scalp in some men later. Acne spots on the face and back are also the result of a sudden excess of testosterone at puberty.

In girls, the FSH stimulates the ovaries to release ova (egg cells) and to produce the female sex hormone oestrogen. The LH causes changes in the ovaries and the secretion of the other female sex hormone, progesterone. Hormones from the ovaries produce physical changes, including the development of the breasts and uterus, the growth of pubic hair and the more rounded female shape.

Hormonal changes bring, in their wake, psychological implications: teenagers will have to manage their increased sexual arousal; parents will have to deal with their offsprings' increased (and, in part, hormone-driven) assertiveness.

In normal boys there is roughly a five-year variation in the age at which puberty is reached. One of the main indicators is ejaculation or emission. By the age of 16, the average boy is fully developed sexually and is capable of becoming a father. The word 'testes' comes from the Latin for 'witness'; for the presence of testicles was a witness to a man's virility and his potential as a father.

GIRLS

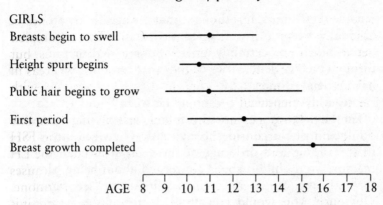

BOYS

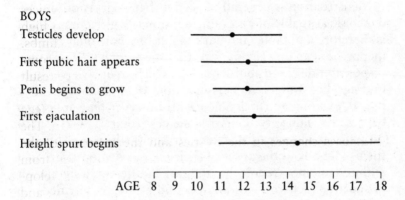

Figure 1 The age range for the onset of physical developments
(● indicates the average age)

The age at which the periods begin varies from country to country. A century ago, the average age for the menarche (the onset of periods) was 14.5 years; today it is around 12 years. Among any group of girls, as I observed earlier, there is great variation. Many will start their periods at 11, 12, 13 or 14 years. A fair number will begin at 10 or 15. A smaller proportion will begin at 9 or 16 years, and a few will even be outside these limits. It is thought that the age of menarche has gradually become lower since Victorian times because of better nutrition: certainly girls who are deficient in iron, through dietary deficiencies or for other reasons, are likely to have a delayed menarche.

Breast development, beginning between 8 and 13 years, is often the first sign of pubescence and early womanhood. But do remember the considerable variation between individuals in the timing and ordering of these physical changes, and reassure your child if she is concerned about being 'slow' or 'behind' the others in their development (see figure 1). Obviously you would consult a doctor if the retardation seemed excessive, or you simply wished to put to rest your own doubts.

Menstruation is generally a signal that a girl is producing ova and is capable of becoming a mother; a girl's first period is therefore a notable landmark in her life. For some girls the menarche is an unwelcome sign that they will have to assume responsibilities and burdens, of which males have little inkling. For others this assumption of womanhood is a proud, exciting and welcome event; however *they* appear to be in the minority. Surveys suggest that a very small proportion of girls (about ten per cent) when asked about their reactions to the onset of their menses demonstrate such enthusiasm; most report that they are indifferent; a significant proportion feel worry or anxiety and a few are terrified.

The growth of breasts can lead to problems for some girls. There are those who are proud of these signs of growing maturity and sexual attractiveness, whereas others attempt to hide them and deny their existence. Such attitudes are often very much influenced by fashion, and the social group to which these young adolescents belong.

Today children are told a great deal more about their approaching puberty than they used to be only a few decades ago. In spite of this, many young adolescents await the first signs of maturity with dread or anxiety. Some boys and girls react adversely to the fact that nocturnal emissions (wet dreams) and menstruation, respectively, happen in a manner that is beyond their control. They may regard these phenomena as shameful in some way, and therefore keep them a secret out of embarrassment. Many of the fears are quite irrational but have their roots in childhood fantasies. The female child might connect menstrual blood with all the horror that goes with a gaping wound; the male child might treat nocturnal emissions with the same disgust as a wet bed. The teenager can so easily regard a normal occurrence with painful embarrassment and guilt that your efforts to keep him or her informed, and to have some helpful books available, should pay handsome 'emotional' dividends.

If the physiological changes of puberty are most commonly taken as the onset of adolescence, it is sociological phenomena, such as status, duties, privileges, the end of education, the right to marry and enjoy economic independence, which are most frequently cited as the termination of adolescence. These matters depend on the conditions and requirements of society. This is our cue to inform ourselves of the means by which selfhood is achieved.

Discovering personal identity

Young people develop a set of feelings and attitudes toward their bodies during adolescence which contribute significantly to their evolving sense of personal identity. These subjective impressions of one's body are referred to as the body image.

The importance of body image to our culture as a whole is obvious in terms of the widespread expenditure of time and effort that is given to altering the body's appearance. Individuals are constantly seeking, by means of clothes, bleaches, skin preparations, cosmetics, tattooing and even plastic surgery, to change their appearance and to make themselves look like some ideal image they have in mind. In some cultures, the need to alter the body's appearance is literally expressed in a whole range of bodily mutilations; members of a culture may radically revise their idealized body image with the passage of time, or under the influential impact of another culture. For example, before the Second

World War, women in Japan adhered to a standard which de-emphasized the breasts. However, as a result of Western influences, there was a radical shift, and it is now a widespread custom for Japanese women to exaggerate breast protuberance in typical American fashion.

'*I know it's a bit late, but looking at our Nigel, I think I'm starting a post-natal depression.*'
Reproduced by permission of *Punch*

Nevertheless, initially, the body image attitudes and distortions produced by normal individuals attracted relatively little interest because they were not as obvious as those manifested by sick and disturbed patients. Although personality theorists developed relatively elaborate formulations concerning an individual's way of organizing perceptions of the behaviour of others, they failed to work out any but the simplest theories about how people organize their perceptions of their own body and how these perceptions affect behaviour.

A child's body perception is modified and gradually extended in the course of development, so as to conform to the current body structure. At the same time, his or her capacities for conceptualization, and for experiencing and interpreting reality, undergo great changes. Children also absorb the attitudes of others towards their body and its parts. They may develop a body concept that is pleasing and satisfying, or they may come to view their body and its parts as offputting, dirty or shameful (see chapter 3).

As I have explained, adolescent self-centredness has its basis in the immense physical changes taking place at puberty. It also has its roots in the discovery of identity, but there are sometimes disconcerting swings from out-and-out narcissism to self-hatred and self-depreciation. And it may be difficult to believe that the same person can be capable of such crass insensitivity at one moment and such thoughtful kindness the next.

When there is a large discrepancy between the teenager's self-concept ('myself as I am') and his or her idealized self ('myself as I would like to be') there is also likely to be anxiety and over-sensitiveness, in close attendance. Being called 'names' such as 'fatty' can hurt, and how others see us and think of us (implicit in those names) is of vital importance to the way we perceive ourselves – our self-image.

The very consequence of being human is that people become objects to themselves, they come to possess an image or idea of what they are like. In terms of evolution, this self-awareness is unique; among the two million or so species that inhabit the earth, humans are the only ones that have developed this characteristic.

The process of discovering the self does not begin or end at adolescence. Rather, one can think of it as a period of heightened awareness of self and an accelerated search for a coherent personal identity. Vinu, writing in late adolescence, has this to say:

Now, while thinking about the 'self', I should not forget that my goal is to attain knowledge, or, in other words, 'know myself'. This goal is obviously very difficult to reach. However, I must try to reach this goal in whatever way possible, intellectually, physically, or through mysticism. . . . To me the most valuable theory in life is knowledge of the self.

Teenagers' perception of their appearance to a particular group of other people, or a particular and significant individual, constitutes a major ingredient of their 'personal identity'. It contains elements of how they wish to be seen by other people. They might be said to have as many identities as there are groups or significant individuals who they believe have a distinctive way of perceiving them.

How youngsters see themselves therefore depends not only on how others see them but on how they *think* others see them – which could, of course, be different from the way in which they are actually perceived. Most particularly, children accept into their self-image what they believe to be their parents' view of them; and these views have consequences, over the long term, for their behaviour. If your son or daughter believes that your opinion is negative or critical (even if this is not really the case), he or she may exhibit insecurity and low self-esteem. The aphorism, 'if people believe things to be real, they are real in their consequences', applies with force to the delicate area of a person's self-image. Young people whose self-esteem is very low tend to be maladjusted in some way.

A popular belief about adolescence is that a crisis over personal identity occurs, producing all or some of the symptoms of stress: anxiety, depression, a sense of frustration, conflict and defeatism. The development of identity doesn't always proceed smoothly, but what evidence we have calls into question the belief of the influential developmental psychologist, Erik Erikson, that adolescents usually suffer a crisis over their identity. Most teenagers actually have a positive but not unrealistically inflated self-image; this view of themselves also tends to be fairly stable over the years.

All this does not mean a complete absence of change during adolescence in teenagers' view of themselves or their ideas about various life issues. Anxieties about the future may increase during the adolescent period – and one might well comment that high unemployment and the threat of nuclear war provide a lot to be anxious about.

It is worth knowing about Erik Erikson's views, since they have been influential. Erikson (in his 1965 and 1968 studies) sees adolescence as one of a sequence of stages in the life-cycle with (like the earlier and later ones) a particular challenge or task to be met. For the teenager it is the challenge between 'identity' and 'identity diffusion' – in a sense, one set against the other (see figure 2). In leaving behind their childish roles (stage 1), adolescents are thought to become preoccupied with finding for themselves a satis-factory answer to the question 'Who am I?' They may 'try out' a variety of identities in their search for answers; they seek experience in different roles and through a variety of relationships (stage 2). It is self-exploration through experi-mentation. Some settle for an immature self too soon ('foreclosure'). Others are too late; thus it is suggested that if boys and girls fail to clarify and give substance to their personal identity they are likely to experience depression and even despair. These feelings, plus a sense of meaninglessness and self-depreciation, are the indications of what Erikson calls 'identity diffusion'. Of course, many of us never cease questioning our identity and elaborating or reshaping our personalities, but we enjoy the security of a clear sense of who we are (stage 3). Figure 2 is an adaptation of Erikson's ideas about the vicissitudes of identity development, put in the form of a flow chart.

Samuel Butler, in *The Way of All Flesh*, wrote:

> All our lives long, every day and every hour, we are engaged in the process of accommodating our changed and unchanged selves to changed and unchanged surroundings; living, in fact, is nothing else than this process of accommodation . . .

Change and accommodation must have some point – a destination and thus a direction. Only parents and adolescents

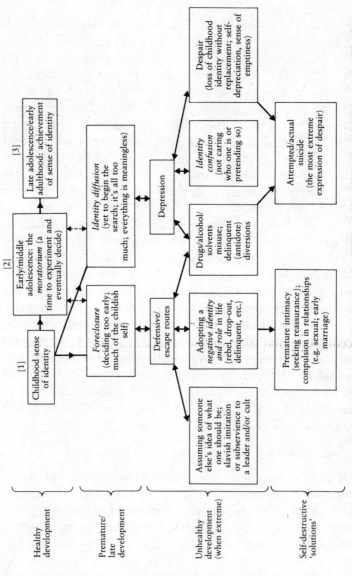

Figure 2 *Stages of identity development (adapted from E. H. Erikson (1965),* Childhood and Society, *London: Chatto and Windus: The Hogarth Press)*

Healthy development }
Premature/ late development }
Unhealthy development (when extreme) }
Self-destructive 'solutions' }

[1] Childhood sense of identity

[2] Early/middle adolescence: the *moratorium* (a time to experiment and eventually decide)

[3] Late adolescence/early adulthood: achievement of sense of identity

Foreclosure (deciding too early; much of the childish self)

Identity diffusion (yet to begin the search; it's all too much; everything is meaningless)

Defensive/ escape routes

Assuming someone else's idea of what one should be; slavish imitation or subservience to a leader and/or cult

Adopting a *negative identity and role* in life (rebel, drop-out, delinquent, etc.)

Drugs/alcohol/ solvents misuse; delinquent (antidote) diversions

Depression

Identity confusion (not caring who one is or pretending so)

Despair (loss of childhood identity without replacement; self-depreciation, sense of emptiness)

Premature intimacy (seeking reassurance); compulsion in relationships (e.g. sexual; early marriage)

Attempted/actual suicide (the most extreme expression of despair)

can decide on their aspirations, but here is a list of personal attributes generally agreed to be positive ones:

1 developing a point of view; one's own outlook on things; being oneself and capable of action and thought;
2 having a sense of humour;
3 accepting reality;
4 accepting oneself, showing respect and liking (not narcissistic self-love) for oneself, plus self-awareness;
5 enjoying human relationships, being capable of forming emotional attachments;
6 showing some concern for social problems (accepting the obligations and duties of being in a social environment);
7 being able to tolerate a certain amount of solitude;
8 respecting other people's view and rights;
9 working out for oneself many of one's own values; not passively accepting conventional wisdom at all times;
10 being flexible in the face of new situations, and capable of changing.

For many people a spiritual or religious dimension is an important element of their identity and lifestyle. Only a small minority of teenagers at 14 and 15 years of age (about 10–12 per cent) state that they do not believe in a god, according to recent British surveys. The remainder have attitudes ranging from 'unsure' to 'definite' belief. They are often fascinated by religious issues and the variety of beliefs, rituals and faiths in the world. This early phase of adolescence, with its relative open-mindedness about religious belief, may lead in some to a religious awakening and a lifetime commitment to worship in one faith or another. Others experience doubt, which may lead to a lifetime of passionate repudiation of any theist interpretation of life, or, more likely, an indifference to, or vagueness about, the spiritual dimension of existence.

Shifts in belief are related to changes in adolescents' cognitive development towards logical and rational modes of thinking. Many teenagers' repudiation of religion is based on a mixture of intellectual, emotional and moral arguments and rationalizations. Words like 'unbelievable', 'reactionary' and 'hypocritical' often come up in debates and discussion. What often happens is that a high proportion will drift back to their early beliefs (if not active churchgoing) after a period of agnosticism or atheism.

A large majority of young teenagers find religious education and church services boring; and there are signs of an increase of negative feelings toward religion – all of which does not augur well for those who wish to promote a religious identity in young people.

Strategies of self-defence

All human beings mature enough to have acquired even a rudimentary self-image need to perceive themselves in a reasonably favourable light. Parents and teachers, by what they say, contribute to the teenager's sense of self-worth. The desire for an acceptable self-image, as a general characteristic of the development of the healthy adolescent, appears to be one of the most critical and significant motivating factors in his or her behaviour. This image can be so highly valued that survival itself (adolescence is a time of heightened risk of attempted suicide) may be valued less than the maintenance of a self-image that has respect and pride associated with it.

Children will obviously be distressed when adults they like are incessantly and unrelievedly critical of them. Any threat to the self's valuation and function is a vital threat to the very being of the individual. As a result, from early in life children acquire complex coping or defensive strategies. These help to soften anxieties and failures and protect the integrity of the self by increasing the feeling of personal worth. To a very great extent we are unconscious of the way we use these strategies. One of the purposes of adopting particular strategies is to reduce tension. The minimizing of immediate discomfort reinforces their use. An individual makes choices and carries out actions which will reduce and, if possible, avoid anxiety, pain or any other distress.

There is evidence that all of us learn to use strategies such as these. It is when we use them inappropriately or to excess, with too great intensity or too inflexibly, that they become (and are called) neurotic. It is the frequency and extent to which we use defensive strategies which is the key to their maladaptiveness. The trouble is that they involve a certain amount of self-deception and distortion of reality and may prevent, by a sort of short-circuiting, the realistic and painstaking solution of problems.

Let us look at some of our psychological strategies. They may aid you in understanding your teenager's behaviour.

1 *Emotional insulation, isolation.* In all these coping strategies the individual reduces the tensions of need and anxiety by withdrawing into a shell of numbness and passivity. One may do this by lowering one's expectations, by remaining emotionally uninvolved and detached. Apathy and defeated resignation may be the extreme reactions to stress and frustration of long duration. Cynicism is often adopted by adolescents as a means of protecting themselves from the pain of seeing idealistic hopes disillusioned.

2 *Escapism (denial of reality).* We may evade disagreeable facts of life by refusing to see them. Escapism is a way of denying unpleasant circumstances. We may simply withdraw from competitive situations if we feel we are at a disadvantage and may fail. An adolescent may escape by getting 'sick' at exam times or may tend to be indecisive and procrastinate in times of stress, putting off the actions that have to be faced realistically.

3 *Fantasy.* Fantasy is one of the favourite tactics of adolescents. Fantasy solutions gloss over unpleasant reality. Teenagers who daydream a lot may be trying to compensate for, or escape from, unacceptable environmental realities. In order to cope with stressful circumstances, they not only deny unpleasant reality but also create the sort of world of fantasy they would like to inhabit. Incidentally, fantasy also provides the opportunity to rehearse in imagination the solutions to their problems without entailing the risks of the real situation; it can be productive in such cases. Non-productive fantasy is the too persistent indulgence in a wish-fulfilling kind of mental activity. The 'Walter Mitty' fantasies allow a

person to be the conquering hero he or she would like to be. People may also explain away their failures and inadequacies by what are called 'suffering hero' fantasies – seeing themselves as misunderstood, 'put-upon', but nobly courageous victims. In this way individuals retain their self-esteem.

4 *Rationalization*. Rationalization helps us to justify what we do and to accept the disappointments arising from unattainable goals. The teenager may use rationalization to modify otherwise unacceptable impulses, needs, feelings and motives into ones which are consciously tolerable and acceptable.

Rationalization helps to reduce 'cognitive dissonance'; when there is a discrepancy between behaviours and thoughts (cognitions), psychological distress is caused. This distress will persist until the behaviours and cognitions are made harmonious again. Students who see themselves as brilliant but do badly in exams may say to themselves that the entire examination system is unreliable and disadvantageous to someone with their highly strung temperament. By this rationalization the gap between their estimation of themselves and their performance disappears; it makes the repugnant more acceptable and the incompatible compatible. So it involves thinking up logical, socially approved reasons for what we have done in the past, are doing now or intend to do in the future.

It is largely an unconscious process, through which we can have our cake and eat it. Common rationalizations are called 'sour grapes' and 'sweet lemons' attitudes. In the former we justify failure to obtain something that is desirable on the grounds that it was not really worthwhile after all. In the 'sweet lemons' attitude we mollify ourselves by saying that it was for our own good in the long run anyway.

5 *Projection*. When feelings arising from within ourselves are unjustifiably attributed to others (projection), it helps us to avoid conflict over our own barely conscious or acknowledged feelings. We let ourselves off the hook by finding

scapegoats and ascribing these obnoxious, intolerable and therefore unacceptable ideas to them. By disowning these tendencies we protect ourselves from anxiety. A girl who feels jealousy and hostility towards her schoolmate may deny these feelings to herself but complain bitterly that her fellow student is unpleasant to her and dislikes her.

6 *Displacement.* Displacement involves a displacement of emotion or an intended action from the person towards whom it was originally intended on to another person or object. An extreme example would be a boy who terrorizes and bullies his peers at school and harasses the teacher in a variety of ingenious and disruptive ways. Investigation might reveal that the causes reside (at least in part) in the home situation, where he is the scapegoat for a bullying and drunken father.

These defensive strategies are not without experimental confirmation. These ideas will come into their own when you are working out the function (or meaning) of adolescents' behaviour seen from their own point of view, even when they are unaware of the reasons for behaving in this way, or cannot articulate them.

Chapter Two

Leaving childhood behind: independence versus authority

Children are travellers newly arrived in a strange country of which they know nothing.

(John Locke)

The struggle for independence

Concern for the inexperience of children entering the realm of adults makes parents protective, sometimes overprotective. There is also a fear, perfectly natural and understandable, that they will 'lose' their children as they grow up. In *Caring for your Children* I traced the child's developing independence and likened it to a spaceship, which has to force itself out of the earth's gravitational pull in order to make its journey. The child must move out of the safe orbit around the mother and strike out to find his or her own place in the world. The adolescent is taking this journey a stage further by moving more and more out of the family orbit.

By the middle years of adolescence this striving for independence is no longer simply one aspect of a youngster's activities; it is, in a very real sense, an end in itself. It involves striving for psychological freedom from parents – freedom to be one's own person, to have one's own thoughts and feelings, to determine one's own values and to plan one's own future, at the broadest existential level. It is also about the more mundane freedoms, to find the clothes, companions and pastimes of one's own choice and to enjoy the privacy of one's own room and belongings.

However, there are as many dangers in granting independence to young people (by promoting too much freedom too soon) as in strongly opposing all signs of it until late adolescence. You may be misled because (say) your son looks more mature than he really is in a physical sense; or your daughter looks less grown-up than she actually is. Being inconsistent, by 'letting go' and then 'holding on' at different and unpredictable times, leads to conflict. Naturally you wish to play a nurturing, protective parental role, being aware of some of the difficulties that lie ahead. Fortunately, the hurdles do not all come together, but tend to be spaced out over the half-dozen or so years of adolescence.

You can smooth the path from childhood to adulthood by supporting your youngster's search for his or her adult role. You should, in the longer term, reap a harvest of goodwill if you are prepared to give your teenager responsibility, the opportunity to play a part in the making of decisions and the formulation of rules. The psychologist Erik Erikson believes that individuals who towards the end of adolescence have achieved a coherent sense of identity feel that they belong to their group. They 'know where they are going'; their past has meaning in terms of their future, and vice versa. One of the reasons why adolescent development is (relatively speaking) so unremarkable in the personal disturbance it causes – and this *is* reassuring – is that there are many strength-giving continuities in this development.

The adolescent builds on what has gone before. Coping skills developed when younger are not necessarily redundant. The distinguished child psychiatrist Professor Michael Rutter, in a 1979 study, makes the point, too, that many of the changes of this stage of development represent pluses, not minuses. They take the form of increased *capacities* of various kinds. It is as well to remember these pluses when considering how much to 'let go'. Research studies indicate that cognitive skills in adolescence become more complete and more flexible as new powers of abstraction and logic make problem-solving easier than it was in childhood. Social skills increase in range and complexity and, indeed, the powers of love and friendship expand and mature. The adolescent's emotional development includes an enhanced ability to appreciate and even respect other people's feelings and to understand their point of view. Whether this ability is put into practice may depend on what may seem to parents like whimsical considerations.

The relationship between parents and teenagers is often a greater problem for the former than the latter. For those parents who are unwilling (or unable) to let their offspring break away from them, or those who, in unhappy or broken marriages, invest all their devotion in their children, adolescence may prove an ordeal. By trying to postpone the inevitable 'weaning' process you can precipitate an abrupt break, or aggravate what should be a relatively painless and gradual loosening of bonds. Both sides become angry and recriminations and guilt feelings may generate a lasting bitterness.

Of course there are also young people who are reluctant to untie the emotional equivalent of the umbilical cord; they hesitate to strike out on their own by accepting the challenge of autonomy. An extreme fear of 'freedom' probably has its roots in childhood. Although parental influence on dependent attitudes and postures is important, it is almost impossible to predict future *adult* dependency from the way in which young children demonstrate such attributes. Adult characteristics of dependency are more reliably predicted from the manner in which adolescents behave. Girls are less likely to change, over the years, than boys; it is somewhat easier to see the continuities in their personal characteristics from childhood through to adulthood, and to predict some of their later behavioural repertoire. Thus it is possible (within broad limits) to anticipate that girls who are passive and dependent during middle and late childhood are likely to show a continuing dependent relationship with their parents, a tendency to withdraw from stress and to avoid risks, during their adult years.

An American psychologist J. Youniss (in his 1980 study) shows that, when older adolescents are psychologically preparing to leave home, they have reached a point when the family is serving as a sort of 'launching centre'. College students who are only part-time residents at home, on occasional weekends and during vacations, illustrate this launching-centre aspect of the family cycle particularly well. This phase represents the culmination of developmental changes which occur in relationships between adolescents and their parents. The psychological reactions of young men who left home to live at college have been compared to the reactions of those of a similar age who continued to live at home while commuting to college. These students were pre-tested while they were still at school, and then retested during their first term of college.

The students were asked about their perceptions of their own and their parents' feelings about affection, communication and independence. For example, affection was indicated by the degree to which the student believed his parents (a) told their friends about him, (b) hugged or kissed him, (c) got on his nerves and (d) enjoyed talking to him; and the degree to which he perceived that he (e) enjoyed talking to them, (f) got on their nerves, (g) felt embarrassed by them and (h) felt uncomfortable being alone with them. Questions were administered twice: in the last year of school and in the first year of college.

The boarders, who had made a more complete break with their families, felt that they and their parents showed more affection after the separation. They also experienced more independence, relative to the commuter group. Thus separation between adolescents and parents seems to be a positive step, with positive psychological reactions, at least for those adolescents who go on to college. In addition, the separation from adolescent children may have positive effects for parents as well. Research indicates that it is in the phase when children have left the parents' home that marital satisfaction is greatest (although there are exceptions to this generalization).

Attachment between parent and child is part of a two-way traffic; both parties may be eager to 'hold on' to each other (inappropriately) or to 'let go' at the right time, or they may be at loggerheads about how and when the youngster should make his or her bid for independence, and in what areas. Independence is not a monolithic 'thing' to be attained all at once.

Parental authority and permissiveness

Studies of parent–child relationships have been made possible by using special psychological measures and statistical techniques to reduce the rich variety of parental attitudes to a few main dimensions. For example there are

(a) attitudes which are 'warm' (or loving) at one extreme, and 'rejecting' (or hostile) at the other;
(b) attitudes which are 'restrictive' (controlling) at one extreme, and 'permissive' (encouraging autonomy) at the other.

The combination of loving and controlling is indicated by behaviours which are restrictive, overprotective, possessive or over-indulgent in content; loving and permissive attitudes are manifest in actions which are accepting, co-operative and democratic. The combination of rejecting and controlling attitudes is exhibited by behaviours which are authoritarian, dictatorial, demanding or antagonistic; rejecting and permissive attitudes are indicated by actions which are detached, indifferent, neglectful or hostile (see figure 3).

The statistical associations are trends only; there is nothing absolute in the relationship between parental attitudes and behaviour. Many authoritarian parents enforce their strict rules in a rather punitive manner, but others do so in a more reasoned and discussive style. Some parents are authoritarian with their daughters but not their sons. The relationships are complex and multifaceted, and this should be borne in mind in the following discussion.

I have suggested that parents have a marked effect on their offspring's striving for independence. The healthy development of autonomy from parents varies according to the type

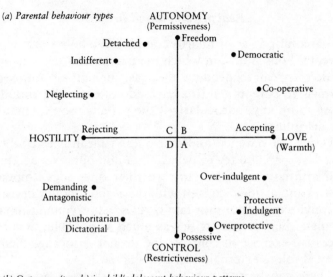

(a) Paridental behaviour types

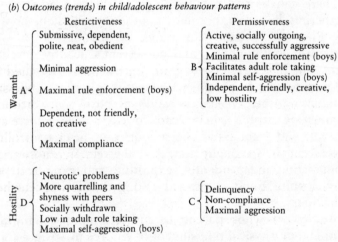

(b) Outcomes (trends) in child/adolescent behaviour patterns

Figure 3   The range of parental behaviour types and their
outcomes within two major dimensions (a) based on the circumplex
model in E. S. Schaefer (1959), A circumplex model for maternal
behaviour, Journal of Abnormal Social Psychology, 59, 226–35,
copyright © 1959 by the American Psychological Association.
Adapted by permission of the author (b) based on W. C. Becker
(1964), 'Consequences of different kinds of parental discipline', in
M. L. Hoffman and L. W. Hoffman (eds) Review of Child
Development Research, vol. 1, New York: Russell Sage
Foundation)

of parental power ordinarily found in the home. Autocratic parental households, in which the parent 'just tells me what to do', appear to produce the least amount of autonomy. Permissive parents tend to have adolescents who show the most autonomy, particularly if the parents use explanations for discipline.

Permissive parents (and that doesn't mean lax, 'couldn't-care-less' parents) try to behave in a non-punitive, accepting and affirmative manner toward their offsprings' impulses, desires and actions; consult with them about policy decisions and give explanations for family rules; allow young people to regulate their own activities as much as possible; avoid the excessive exercise of control; and do not encourage them to obey absolute externally defined standards.

There can be too much of a good thing, a point when mothering, in excess, becomes smothering; the same applies to fathering. Parental nurturance is undoubtedly a vital ingredient in the child's and adolescent's healthy development, but as with everything *moderation* is the watchword.

Overprotective parents frequently alternate between dominating their teenagers and submitting to them. A dominating attitude may lead to excessively dependent, passive and submissive behaviour on the part of the adolescent. It is thought that, if youngsters are discouraged from acting independently, exploring and experimenting, they acquire timid, awkward and generally apprehensive behaviours.

Adolescents whose parents are authoritarian and of the type who favour physical punishment to enforce their rigid set of rules (in which the adolescent has no voice) tend to have more dependent and, at the same time, rebellious adolescent offspring. Restrictive, authoritarian parents attempt to shape, control and assess the behaviour and attitudes of the child according to a set code of conduct, usually an absolute standard, which is often motivated by religious considerations. Obedience is valued as a virtue, and punitive, forceful measures are usually favoured in order to curb self-will at those points where the child's (and later on, the teenager's) actions or beliefs conflict with what parents think is correct conduct. They believe in *indoctrinating* – as opposed to educating – their offspring into such values as respect for authority, respect for work, and respect for the preservation of traditional order. Verbal exchange is discouraged because the teenager should accept the parent's word for what is right.

The children of domineering parents often lack self-reliance and the ability to cope realistically with their problems; later they may fail or prove slow to accept adult responsibilities. They are apt to withdraw from situations they find difficult, and they tend to be the people who later make up most of that part of the adult world which has never left home, psychologically and, much of the time, physically as well.

At the opposite extreme are parents whose concern is minimal and whose attitudes to the child are casual, *laissez-faire*, lax or even indifferent. Psychological independence may be put at risk if parents reject their offspring. For some adolescents, rejection means callous and indifferent neglect or positive hostility from the parents; but it may also be emotional and subtle. Teenagers come to believe that they are worthless, that their very existence makes their parents unhappy.

A rejecting parent may not only ignore the offspring's need for nurturance but also punish manifestations of that need. One would expect, therefore, that more severe forms of rejection would lead the youngster to suppress such behaviour. When, on the other hand, parents withhold or are sparing with their attention and care, but do not actually punish dependent behaviour, they are likely to intensify adolescent needs for attention and care. The more a youngster is 'pushed away' (figuratively speaking), the more he or she clings.

Most parents 'interfere' in, or (as they would prefer to call it) 'guide', the choices and activities of their children. In extreme cases, according to some theorists, verbal interactions between such parents and their children tend to be stereotyped, with almost no outlet for spontaneous expression. Frequently they fail to respond to their offsprings' communications or to their demands for a recognition of their own point of view. The parents' statements tend to be intrusive and take the form of interventions rather than replies. The replies they do make tend to be selective responses to those of the youngster's expressions which have been initiated by themselves rather than to any expressions originated by him or her. Spontaneous utterances and self-expression are restricted, as if the young person were being denied the right to an independent point of view.

Research into childrearing techniques suggests the need for an approach which is not always easy for parents (even if they agree in principle) to achieve in practice. A judicious blend of permissivenes and a warm, encouraging and accepting attitude fits the recommendations of childrearing specialists who are concerned with fostering the sort of young people who are socially outgoing, friendly, creative and reasonably independent and self-assertive. Certainly, we know that the extremes of permissiveness and restrictiveness entail risks. Teenagers with warm, permissive parents, if brought up and trained mainly through love, good models to identify with and imitate, and the giving of reasons, are provided with the opportunity to learn for themselves (by trial and error). Parents who are authoritative, rather than authoritarian, attempt to direct their child's activities in a rational manner determined by the issues involved in particular questions of discipline. They encourage verbal exchange, and share with the youngster the basic reasoning behind their policy.

Such democratic interactions characterize the households of adolescents who are a psychologically 'healthier' set of individuals, who are able to strike off on their own in adulthood. Such well-adjusted families are able to engage in conflict while still maintaining levels of warmth and dominance not of the heavy-handed variety. Perhaps an ability to deal with increased conflict without withdrawing affection or becoming authoritarian is one reason why these families have, in general, coped successfully with various life problems.

Many families who seek help from psychologists are worried about conflicts over the granting of autonomy to adolescents. Typically the adolescents want independence to do things such as smoke, select their own clothes, go to bed when it suits them, at a younger age than the parents are prepared to accept. Parents will often ask psychologists to give some indication of what most parents and adolescents believe are appropriate ages for the granting of autonomy to adolescents for the various issues discussed. Since these are difficult questions to answer because they involve personal values rather than 'scientific facts', I suggest you have a go at the questionnaire below.

In the columns indicate at what age you think boys and girls should be allowed to:

		Boys	Girls
1	Go shopping to a large complex without their parents	. . . .	
2	Decide when they should leave school	. . . .	
3	Decide what food they eat	. . . .	
4	Decide what time they go to bed	. . . .	
5	Drink alcohol if they want it	. . . .	
6	Decide which television programmes they watch	. . . .	
7	Go out with a boyfriend/girlfriend if they want to (dating)	. . . .	
8	Decide what school they will go to	. . . .	
9	Decide which clothes they will wear	. . . .	
10	Decide which films they can go to see	. . . .	
11	Decide what time they should come home at night	. . . .	
12	Smoke if they want to	. . . .	

Dr A. Hudson and colleagues in Australia collected information in 1985 on these questions from many hundred parents and secondary school pupils. You might like to compare your answers with answers given by your friends and your child. Their study demonstrated that families vary quite considerably about what age is appropriate to do X, Y or Z. Middle-class parents and teenagers will expect the youngster to make his or her own decisions at slightly earlier ages than working-class parents and adolescents. Conflict is more likely to occur after children are 13 years old, when they come to believe that independence should be granted at earlier ages; and older parents and fathers (generally) will tend to wish for a delay in granting such autonomy.

You might bear in mind that disagreements about rules are bound to occur in the thrust towards independence. Your teenager no longer thinks like a child. Intellectual growth shows a fairly steep rise during the early years of adolescence but with decreasing steepness until its ultimate growth is attained (in the early twenties). The most notable advance in such cognitive functioning (as it is called) is the emergence at about the age of 12 of what is called formal-operational reasoning: the ability to think hypothetically, to imagine a range of possibilities and future events, and to think systematically about one's own thought processes. To put it another way, adolescents are capable of rational, abstract thought.

Not surprisingly, young people begin to flex their intellectual muscles by using their new powers of reasoning to be critical or sceptical about cherished parental beliefs and values, not to mention those well-meant rules.

A psychoanalyst Martha Harris makes the point (in a 1969 study) that bringing up adolescents implies being willing to review one's own rules, standards and judgements, as well as to criticize theirs. You can only expect to educate them by re-educating yourself. This does not, of course, mean acquiescing to all their opinions and giving up all your own dislikes to adapt to theirs. On the contrary – no growth is possible this way.

But reviewing opinion entails discussion. It means agreeing, even if only agreeing to differ, having considered the arguments and the evidence. Confidence for the teenager comes not only from experience but from evaluating the experience, thinking about it and exchanging ideas about it in discussions with friends and family.

Teenagers often come to agree with parents' attitudes and values. Debby, a late adolescent, put it like this:

> Up to a certain age I believed everything my parents said. Then, in college, I saw all these new ideas and I said, 'Okay, I'm not going to believe all that stuff you told me', and I rejected everything and said to myself, 'Okay, now I'm going to make a new Debby which has nothing to do with mother and father. I'm going to start with a clean slate', and what I started to put on were all new ideas. These ideas were opposite to what my parents believed. But slowly, what's happening is that I'm adding on a lot of things which they told me and I'm taking them as my own and I'm coming together with them.

Settling differences

The organizers of an Open University course entitled *Parents and Teenagers* have suggested a step-by-step approach to settling differences of opinion between parents and adolescents. Let us take the example that parents often mention to me: a clash with a teenager son who wishes to buy a motor cycle against his mother's wishes.

1 Try and work out your own attitudes and feelings about the situation before you approach your son. Completing this sentence can help you to clarify it in your mind:

    (a) I feel . . . (describe your feeling – angry, afraid, etc.)
    (b) when he . . . (describe the situation, e.g. talks about buying a motor cycle)
    (c) because . . . (describe why you feel that way).

2 Decide whether the particular situation is worth having all this bother for. List several reasons why the issue is worth

raising, *and* why it may not. Rate your reasons on the star system (* * * * meaning very important; * meaning trivial). Do the reasons for tackling the issue outweigh the reasons against, or is it finely balanced? The example above might go like this:

Reasons for talking to my son about the wisdom of buying a motor bike:

He may be injured or killed (there is a high risk). * * * *
He can't really afford it. * *
Motor bikes are associated with rather rough types. *

Reasons against:

There'll be another awful row between us. * * *
He'll do as he pleases anyway. *
He needs some transport and he certainly can't afford a car. * *

3 Decide on the spirit in which you will raise the matter. For example, I want to deal with it . . . (firmly, forcefully, mildly, etc.).

4 Approach your teenager.

(a) Begin by telling him how you feel, and why (see step 1).
(b) Avoid expressing your feeling as criticisms or attacks which will make him defensive and/or aggressive.

5 Listen to his reply and check your understanding of:

(a) his feelings about the situation; and
(b) his reasons for them.

Say: 'You feel . . . because . . .' and see if you have his point of view clear in your mind.

6 Work out a practical agreement/compromise, if you can. It may be difficult, sometimes impossible; but it is more likely that you'll find a solution if you acknowledge his feelings, explain yours, and discuss matters quietly and calmly, and with goodwill.

This particular example is a difficult one for parents to resolve because a compromise is not easy, and also because of the risk involved. Parents are proud (even pleased) when younger children are daring, even though they may feel worried (say) at the height of the tree climbed or the speed with which the bike is ridden. Teenagers will take risks; they are a necessary part of adolescent experimentation. But the risks are sometimes too high, and the judgement (and experience) of the adolescent too limited, to allow parents to acquiesce in their activities.

Parents typically list the following risks that cause them worry: that he or she will be in an accident; be killed; be assaulted/raped; get into a fight; get into trouble with authority (teachers, police); get a girl pregnant/get pregnant; harm himself/herself; harm someone else; try out and succumb to drugs; make the wrong choice of partner.

You might try out an exercise (in your mind) in settling differences with your child, where the risks are not so high and/or the chances of compromise are greater.

1 Your teenager wants to throw a party and has asked you to go out or stay with a relative for the night.
2 Your child wishes to come home at 2 p.m. and you prefer some time before midnight.
3 You disapprove of the boy/girl your teenager is going out with because of their bad reputation.

There are various ways in which parents can discuss these issues with their offspring.

The authors of the *Parents and Teenagers* course suggest that you will achieve a better perspective if you ask yourself what risks *you* took at that age.

Think back for a moment to your own adolescence.
Tick which of the following you tried at any time:
Smoking more than five cigarettes a day   □
Drinking beer more than three times a week   □
Drinking spirits regularly   □
Riding a motor bike   □
Hitch-hiking   □

Staying at a party all night ☐
Mountain-climbing/pot-holing with a friend ☐
Trying marijuana ☐
Going on a crash diet ☐
Sniffing glue or other solvent ☐
Having sex without using a contraceptive ☐ .
Riding a bicycle in a busy street ☐

They provide the following ground-rules for the ensuing conversation. Work out what is at stake. Deciding whether or not to take (or sanction) a risk depends on:

1 How likely you believe the feared outcome might be.
2 How important/damaging the possible outcome is.
3 How much you/your teenager have to lose.

You need to:

1 Remember that risk-taking is an important (if worrying) feature of adolescent development.
2 Ensure that you and your teenager are well informed (e.g. that a potential motorbike rider has a good machine and is well trained in driving and roadcraft).
3 Model your preferred way of life (e.g. if you warn them that smoking is hazardous, refrain from smoking yourself).
4 Discuss risk-taking with your son or daughter. Try to agree what he or she can do to make the experimenting relatively safe. Think about what you can do to make it so.
5 Negotiate and bargain if necessary (there is a section on agreements and contracts in chapter 10). You may reach a compromise or give way on one (lesser) risk so as to obtain your teenager's agreement to forgo another one.
6 Do not pry. Your teenager should be able to manage most risks unaided. But make it clear that there are limits; for example, there are behaviours such as obsessive anorexic dieting where you would not hesitate to seek help. If an aggressively drunk group of adolescents gatecrashed a party or a youngster introduced drugs, you would call the police. So don't meddle, but make the ground-rules plain and stark.

7 Remember that your ultimate goal is for your teenager to be self-directed – to manage his or her own health and life.

Adolescent rebellion and conformity

In city environments, pre-adolescent children and (especially) young adolescents are tending to acquire their values more and more from outside the family; their peers to some extent tend to replace the parents as interpreters and enforcers of the moral code. This is especially so – according to some writers on adolescence – now that we live in a period of rapid social change and rapid communication. Changes in attitudes and values are so quick to occur and so radical in nature that we get (or so it is claimed) a hiatus between one generation and the next. Such an alienation between parent–child generations when it does occur is bound to add to the role of peer groups in the process of socialization.

You may have been led to believe that 'distancing' of teenagers from their parents is almost inevitable, and you may be expecting not to be able to communicate with your children when they get older. Alienation is not, however, a typical pattern. Most adolescents are still attached to their homes in a positive way, and they continue to depend upon the emotional support, goodwill and approval of their parents. The family continues to be of critical importance to them as it was in earlier, less mature years; indeed, your concern and supervision (as long as it is not oppressive, or too intrusive) is vital during a phase when youngsters are experimenting with life.

Although the evidence is meagre, it does appear that rebelliousness and alienation are more likely in teenagers who, in spite of considerable maturity, remain economically or in other ways, dependent on their parents – such as students in higher education.

A majority of adolescents share their parents' attitudes towards moral and political issues, and are prepared (by and large) to accept their parents' guidance on academic, career and personal issues. If anything, the generations are drawing together rather than apart. Teenagers and their parents tend to agree on the important issues more than do parents and *their* parents (grandparents). Of course there are exceptions to the general rule; but, even where the rule does apply, exceptions occur at certain times when disagreements flare up. (At what age aren't there any conflicts?) But the generation gap does not live up to popular expectations; it is certainly not a chasm. What, in any event, constitutes 'alienation'? Labels are misleading and even dangerous because they suggest distinctions that are absolute rather than matters of degree. There are, of course, important differences between the 'culture' of your family and that of your youngster's peer group, but the evidence suggests that these differences do not necessarily lead to conflict.

It is, in fact, exceptional for teenagers to feel torn between their two 'worlds', certainly on the more important issues of life. There are more likely to be differences of opinion on minor issues such as hairstyle, fashion, social habits and privileges, where you certainly risk having your views rejected in favour of the standards of your youngster's friends.

Where *major* issues are concerned, it seems that only a minority of adolescents radically depart from their parents' views. Contrary to popular belief, there is little evidence that secondary or higher education, in itself, causes changes in the political attitudes that young people absorb from their parents. Students of political attitudes indicate that most teenagers are inclined to show low levels of political participation, minimal political knowledge and considerable apathy and cynicism. Some secondary school students are politically *aware*, with a concern for social issues, but are disenchanted with the political establishment.

It is during later adolescence, but only for a relatively small number (students in higher education, in particular), that youth and idealism combine with the optimistic view that radical change of the social and political system is possible, and that injustice and inequality can be eradicated. The idealism of adolescence has sparked off some of the great reformers of history – men and women who sustained their high ideals throughout life. Every society tends to become blasé, cynical or corrupt, and it is fortunate that, with each new generation, there is a renewal of idealistic enthusiasm.

In some cases, changes in young people's political views result not so much from rational reappraisal as from their need to conform to prevailing ideologies, or as a reaction against parents for whom the adolescent has negative feelings. For other young people, at a stage in their development when they are shedding some old ideas and illusions and assimilating new ones, adolescence is a time when they may reject many of their parents' ideas and attitudes as old-fashioned and reactionary. Others may intensify the idealism they have absorbed from their parents.

The radical, sometimes revolutionary views of young people meet with a variety of response from their parents and teachers – including horror, indifference and sad (or amused) tolerance. Some parents, remembering the idealism they have lost, may mutter cynically to themselves: 'Wait until he has a mortgage and a family.' Professional politicians and other political activists attempt to attract and focus the energies and courage of the young, knowing how important they are for the regeneration and viability of political life.

When young people complain that their parents do not understand them, what they may really be trying to explain, however inarticulately, is the parents' failure to see their idealism. When they lash out, at their parents in particular, and at the world in general, it may be because they perceive the discrepancy between the high standards people talk about and the standards of public and private life which actually exist.

Many adolescents believe that the world can be changed to meet the ideals of their generation; they believe that humanity, freedom and justice are possible, and that there do exist real counterparts to the slogans and idealistic appeals that figure so strongly in their bedroom posters. Some may dream of escape to a better world – a utopian lifestyle among people uncorrupted by materialism and convention. Generally they remain only dreams.

A small number of adolescents do choose to step out of their parents' way of life, and try out radically different lifestyles. They begin to identify with new groups, some eccentric (even deviant) but exciting in their boldness and their novelty. They may be flattered by the acceptance they receive from members of the subculture they join. Such adolescents are thus exposed to some very powerful 'reference' groups – that is, those with whom adolescents identify and from whom they absorb attitudes, values, beliefs and fashions.

Usually it is older teenagers who wish to experiment with new values and lifestyles, and a few may reject life in the conventional nuclear family and seek alternative ways of living together in groups. They may be young people bound together perhaps by a shared political ideology, sometimes by religious belief, or even a predilection for using drugs, but often for a host of other reasons, especially economic ones. Such marked unconventionality is, however, extremely rare. There are many other, more common ways of expressing the desire to be 'outside' conventional society. Punks, with their colourful and unusual hairstyles and clothing, underline their outsider status. So do some football fans.

The most recent public outrage in Britain at the time of writing this book – an outburst accompanied by screaming newspaper headlines and sombre denunciations from politicians, has been generated by football hooliganism. A situation deserving grave public concern is whipped up into a state of hysteria, or what sociologists call moral panic.

It is instructive to look more closely at this phenomenon, since it tends to occur most often in connection with young people and their lifestyle. Thus we have had waves of public criticism aimed at Teddy boys, mods and rockers, hippies and many others. Commentaries about each of these groups of 'outsiders' have been pervaded by an apocalyptic tone. What on earth is happening to society?

Strangely enough, most of these youngsters get older and seem to settle down as 'insiders'; and some of them (doubtless forgetting) can be heard railing against the unspeakable things the next generation of rebels are getting up to.

Peter Marsh, a psychologist at Oxford, has studied British football hooliganism (so called) and finds that, far from being the undifferentiated mass of deviants, yobbos and delinquents the mass media would have us believe them to be, football fans are very varied both as individuals and as subgroups. They have different ranks, each with its special style of dress. They wear a uniform of long scarves in team colours, often tied around the arm rather than the neck, and jackets, trousers and boots of a particular style. There are several subgroupings: boys who have recently joined, older boys who are about to leave, 'hooligans' and 'nutters'. Each wears a variation of the uniform. But the uniform signals their outsider status, their difference from the rest of society, while indicating their solidarity with one another. They regard the 'nutters', who are the real troublemakers, as outsiders from themselves. When the media or police label all noisy, unruly football fans as deviant simply because they are easily recognizable and so tempting to generalize about in their often boorish actions, there is the risk of the phenomenon called deviance amplification. It happened during the 1960s towards the end of the hippy revolution. The stigmatization of young people caused some of them to accept the extreme stereotypes about themselves, and served to cut them off from the rest of society and the normal pressures of social influence.

For the majority of young people, their survival depends on living within the confines of society. However, teenagers gradually become less involved in the family's leisure activities, and more engaged in activities with friends and with groups of peers. None the less, surveys show that most adolescents are more likely to identify with their parents than with their friends.

Adults tend to see adolescents as out-and-out deviants or

nonconformists. But often they are extremely conformist among their own adolescent friends. Researchers have observed that most adolescents must conform among themselves to avoid exclusion, expulsion or ridicule.

Susceptibility to pressure by people of one's own age increases up to about the age of 15 years, and thereafter gradually declines. Conforming people tend to see themselves as well adjusted and extrovert, presumably because, in describing themselves, they try to conform to an image they consider socially desirable.

If the teenager cannot leave the social group that he or she belongs to – and one thinks of the lonely adolescent who cannot find other friends – then there is usually compliance from the individual. However, if he or she wants to be in the clique then there is likely to be private acceptance as well as outward conformity. Conformity is likely to be at its greatest when the limits of the group's tolerance and the penalties for deviance are clearly defined.

Teenagers' expectation of acceptance depends on the degree to which they believe they possess the attributes that their peers value – qualities such as skill, strength, good looks, verbal facility, and so on. The more accepted teenagers are by the group, the more willing they are to conform; the more willing they are to conform, the better accepted they will be.

Willingness to conform is, of course, a desirable attribute only up to a point. Over-socialized youngsters could emerge from a pattern of childrearing rooted in indoctrination. In deciding when conformity becomes excessive, it is necessary to ask to whom and how often the child submits, and in what contexts the child is prepared to conform. Can your son or daughter distinguish (for example) between the reasonable demands you make in the name of their care and training, and the unreasonable coercion of, say, a delinquent gang? Do they stick up for their own rights or point of view, or slavishly accede to the wishes and attitudes of others? It is hoped, in other words, that the youngster will be discriminating, learning to judge between the desirability or undesirability of people, of particular demands and of values (especially moral values).

The point worth remembering, perhaps, is that, although some inter-generational conflict exists, its importance has been greatly exaggerated. One needs to learn the art of treating adolescents as young adults, not because they are yet grown up, but in order to help them become adult. At the same time one is trying to shelter them from the worst consequences of their mistakes, and helping them to cope with the disappointments and setbacks (as well as the triumphs) which are part of growing up.

Parents can no longer rely on 'respect for authority', in the old-fashioned sense, to bring their teenagers into line on this or that issue. The young today wish to know what a person is like *as a person* rather than what his or her status is (be it parent, teacher, boss). They ask themselves whether they like and respect the person. Then they give (or withhold) their obedience, their loyalty, and their willingness to emulate or learn from them.

Making and choosing friends

Parents are naturally concerned about the kinds of friends their children choose, since friends may counteract parental influence. Children belong to two societies: the society of adults and that of their peers. This is particularly so as they approach their teens. Parents rightly concern themselves more, at this stage, about the 'good' and 'bad' influences in their children's lives. They worry about the company they keep, as they grow out of, and away from, the family. One type of group can foster hostile, disobedient, uncreative individuals; another can develop confused, purposeless drifters; and still another produces co-operative, flexible, purposeful, altruistic children. In turn, the atmosphere of the group is determined by the qualities of its leaders and those of the other group members. Research into juvenile mis-behaviour demonstrates the importance of keeping track of what children are doing.

Although friendships should be monitored, the style of doing so is important. Obviously you should not keep your child under unremitting surveillance, but if youngsters are left completely unsupervised they are almost certain to think of ways of getting into trouble. Try to keep a 'low profile'. The type of friend he or she mixes with can be important. And the degree of influence the friends have is usually critical. The balance should not be allowed to tilt too far away from the family, and too far towards the peer group, if you are interested in having a say in your offspring's socialization. Many parents of delinquent children do not care what their children are up to, as long as they themselves are not bothered. It is surely worth the effort to get to know your children's friends and to be aware of the sort of groups or gangs they are associating with.

Friendship is generally defined as a relationship between people who are bound by a common purpose. Not surprisingly, the adolescent who cannot appreciate the reciprocal nature of friendship – the need for mutual understanding, being able to share and to be trusted – is not likely to sustain stable relationships or, indeed, be chosen as a friend. Immature youngsters cannot always manage the give-and-take of friendship.

Adolescents emphasize loyalty and intimacy above all else when they are asked about the essential qualities of friendship. It follows that friendship choices tend to be influenced by similarities in social background, religious affiliations and ethnic-group membership, because the inculcation of similar 'norms' and ideas ensures a certain identity in values and attitudes. The most significant influence on the formation of friendships is the *belief* that another is similar to oneself; this is more important than whether or not he or she is *actually* similar. Individuals also choose as friends those with characteristics considered desirable in terms of the values of their group.

Some children are attracted to others whose needs complement their own, although this is rare. For example, a dominant child may become friendly with someone who is predominantly submissive, but the principle that opposites attract is the exception, not the rule. Research workers have demonstrated that people tend to choose others whom they perceive as choosing *them*. In other words, people like others whom they believe view them in a favourable light.

Youngsters who cannot get on with other children often lead miserable and lonely lives. There is evidence that those who have problems with their peer group early in life tend to have severe difficulties during adolescence and adult life. After all, peer relations are of vital importance for the very reason that they provide opportunities to learn how to interact with others, to control one's social behaviour, to develop interests and skills appropriate to one's age and to share similar feelings and attitudes. The opportunity to reveal oneself, the sense of confidence and the feeling of having something unique and exclusive also provide those intimacies which make friendship so important; their absence (for the friendless adolescent) makes the world seem a cold, inhospitable place to live in.

In a typical classroom, about one young person in five turns out to be an isolate. None of their classmates chooses them as a friend. At the other extreme, most groups have a few popular members, chosen by many of their classmates. It is important to distinguish popularity – general attractiveness to others – from the ability to form *specific* friendships. Popular children may have many admirers but few special friends. Being singled out for admiration by many may even tend to isolate a person from close personal relationships, especially if the qualities or accomplishments which earn popularity are envied by others who lack such gifts.

If you are concerned about your teenager's inability to make or keep friends, carry out a small exercise in 'accountancy'. Look at things from the other person's point of view. Is your teenager being insensitive, too demanding or disloyal? Is his or her company rewarding enough? The ability to make friends requires a certain liking for oneself, as well as a degree of self-awareness and social sensitivity. Self-image plays a part in all of this; if it has been endlessly subverted by

criticism or rejection the adolescent is likely to feel unworthy and inferior and display 'offputting' behaviours which betray defensiveness and over-anxiety.

Young people who are accepted by their peers tend to:

1 demonstrate sensitivity, responsiveness and generosity; they help others and give attention, approval and affection to their peers;
2 be confident in their social contacts, active and friendly;
3 see things from the other youngster's point of view;
4 be good at resolving day-to-day (and difficult) dilemmas involving person-to-person relationships;
5 make others feel accepted and involved, promoting and planning enjoyable group activities;
6 demonstrate empathetic actions: empathy involves the youngster's capacity to control his or her behaviour by considering its effect on the experiences of others, particularly the potential victims of proscribed behaviour.

In middle childhood friendships are fairly unstable; interests change easily at this period, and old friends may be unable to satisfy new needs. The capacity for building lasting friendships gradually increases during childhood and adolescence. As the child grows older, interests become focused, and friendships are thus more likely to be enduring. Below the age of 11 or 12, girls are more socially active than boys, and tend to establish more intimate and confidential relationships with each other. The capacity of the older child to form friendships, and to maintain them on the basis of meeting others' needs as well as his or her own, is thought to be a strong indication of developing social maturity.

During middle childhood and pre-adolescence, the child's relationships tend to be focused on the neighbourhood and same-sex groups or 'gangs'. They tend to be informal at first and then, from the age of 10 years or so, they take on a much more structured organization (such as special membership requirements). Friendships and acquaintances during the pre-adolescent and earliest adolescent years also tend to be restricted, by and large, to members of the same sex.

With the transition from childhood to adulthood, relationships with friends and acquaintances reach new levels of intensity, and they multiply in number. The psychiatrist H. Stack Sullivan, an influential theorist, in a 1953 study describes the change in emphasis in the 'dynamisms' or *needs* of young people as they move from childhood, through preadolescence, and on to adolescence. The first dynamism governing social interaction in infancy and early childhood is the need for security. Feelings of self-worth in the person's interactions and relationships with others of significance (particularly parents) are bound up with this major need. Because children in infancy and early childhood are wholly dependent on others, the potential for anxiety based on insecurity in interpersonal relationships is great.

Later comes 'intimacy' – a need for emotional sharing with others of significance. This phase of childhood represents a time of life when the peer group assumes a greater role in the individual's interpersonal life. Intimacy, the need for emotional sharing, blossoms in the forming of a particularly close relationship with one member of the peer group of the same age and sex. For the first time, the early adolescent experiences sensitivity to what matters to another person, a special friend isolated from the larger same-sex group. Such intense friendships have a special role in the development of emotional intimacy. Studies of student relationships indicate that those students who have a special friend tend to be significantly more altruistic than those students without one. Self-revelation is crucial. As one youngster put it:

A friend is a person you can talk to, you know, show your feelings and she'll talk to you. You can talk more freely to a friend. Someone you can tell your problems to and she'll tell you her problems. They are open. You can tell a friend everything. A friend is a person you can really tell your feelings to; a person you can . . . confide in; tell them what you feel and you can be yourself with them.

The emotional element, to which the term 'friendship' is generally applied, is not of the tender, sentimental or sexual kind. Friendship certainly involves a deep affection (we speak of loving our friends); we often know them intimately and the relationship is lasting. Strong emotions can be freely admitted during pre-adolescence without posturing and without fear of rejection. Adolescence itself is the time for a shift from same-sex intimate friendships to opposite-sex intimate friendships. Following puberty what Sullivan calls the 'lust dynamism' emerges as a major need to be integrated with security and intimacy in a close relationship with a member of the opposite sex.

Sullivan describes as a major theme of personality development the management of anxiety which arises from complex and sometimes difficult social interactions. Adolescence can be a time of stressful social interactions because the individual's needs, security, intimacy and lust come into conflict with one another. Indeed, many adolescents have difficulty integrating these three dynamisms. Their interactions are sometimes unruly and refuse to keep to the neat compartments society assigns for them.

Embarrassment and awkwardness result from the clash between lust and intimacy. Non-sexual or 'platonic' love is the kind that the social norms prescribe for the bonds of friendship. However, significant numbers of young people have experienced sexually or erotically tinged feelings, and, indeed, physical contacts with members of the same sex, without, in any way, being diverted from a primarily heterosexual orientation. Many suffer untold miseries because they have misinterpreted these 'normal' developmental experiences as evidence of incipient sexual deviance.

At this stage, the development of the teenager's sense of identity is embryonic; youngsters identify with others of the same sex – friends and older 'heroes' – sometimes even having a 'crush' on an idealized older pupil or teacher or some other charismatic figure.

As boys and girls enter the wider world of adolescence, the range of 'play' activities (social and sporting) and the circle of acquaintances widen, and they spend much less time at home. Social relationships with peers tend to fall into three broad categories: the larger crowd or set; the more intimate clique; and individual friendships. The crowd is essentially an association of cliques. To belong to a crowd the youngster needs to belong to a clique. Clique members seem to do a lot of talking, especially (as parents' phone bills suggest) on the telephone.

The crowd allows for more organized and larger social activities such as parties, which also provide opportunities for the sexes to mix. As interest in the opposite sex increases, the undercurrents of hostility between the sexes begin to vanish. Heterosexual group activities – in cliques – are common. There is moral support available in these early forays away from mixing only with friends and acquaintances of the same sex. This is a testing ground, so to speak, an opportunity to develop social skills with the opposite sex, to learn about its members.

Chapter Three

Transition: the emotional problems of adolescence

Adolescence can be so difficult. I constantly wonder if there is some way to help you avoid the sadnesses and the troubles, although I know that if I somehow could protect you from experiencing the pain inherent in growing up, you would never be able fully to experience the pleasure nor achieve maturity easily. . . . I fear for you, because I remember so vividly.

(Polly Devlin, writing to her daughter)

Adolescence as a period of transition

Parents are seldom more needed by their children, for emotional support, than at puberty and afterwards. Their parental role will be subtly altered; they have to be much more discreet and indirect in their supervision and nurturance, as the teenager matures.

Adolescence, as a period of dramatic transition, involves many novel experiences and new challenges. Teenagers usually like it both ways: the freedom of an adult and the protection of a child. If parents can walk this tightrope, this stage of adolescent transition can be the most exciting one of all. By keeping in touch with their adolescent children they keep in touch with young people in general, and keep their own ideas flexible and youthful. That tightrope is not so easy if parents have suffered during their own adolescence.

Of course, we do not always like the manner in which teenagers react to transition, or the direction in which change seems to be taking them. Understandably enough, our attitudes are not always objective. Adults often accuse modern youth of being over-indulged, even decadent. They express disdain, yet seem endlessly fascinated by what young people are doing. Perhaps they are envied because they appear to have fun and their lives seem to have an element of excitement. Envy may breed resentment, and resentment gives rise to the sort of projection discussed in chapter 1. We project the troubles of the world (and perhaps the dark side of our natures) upon the young.

Parents are facing shifts at this time in their own personal development, from youthful maturity to early middle age. We cannot consider adolescents and their problems without considering the manner in which they interact with their parents, who are not without their own preoccupations and anxieties.

Most parents are over 30 years old when their first child reaches puberty. Indeed, there are parents whose children reach their teens when they are in their forties or even fifties. And it should be said that it is the prime of life for the fortunate ones. But what do the teenagers make of them – be they in their thirties, forties or fifties? For some (especially if we confirm their views) their parents' generation seems to have lost its zest for living, to be staid and boringly settled, to have lost the freshness of youth. They may believe (patronizingly) that their parents' lives are without passion.

Some people in the middle years of adulthood feel this way themselves. One such had this to say:

the realization suddenly struck me that I had become, perhaps not an old fogy, but surely a middle-aged fogy. For the train was filled with college boys returning from vacation. They cruised up and down the aisles, pretending to be drunk ... boisterous, but not obnoxious; looking for fun, but not for trouble. Yet most of the adult passengers were annoyed with them, including myself. I sat there, feeling a little like Eliot's Prufrock, 'so meticulously composed, buttoned-up, bespectacled, mouth thinly set'.

Parents sometimes create their own problems by trying to live through their children, relying mainly on vicarious satisfactions. In this context, it is commonly asserted that middle age is a more difficult phase of life for mothers than fathers. The changes in a mother's life are in many ways more obvious. The children are becoming less dependent, if not totally independent, of her; and until this period of her life her maternal interests may have been uppermost in her life. Although her concern continues, her direct role as a mother is coming to an end. But conventional wisdom does exaggerate the 'empty nest' phenomenon. Most middle-aged women do think about the approaching departure of their youngest child, about to leave secondary school, as a forthcoming change in their lives; but they do not consciously anticipate a difficult time for themselves. A majority of men ignore this imminent event in their lives, and seem much more pre-occupied with their own retirement in the future.

Francis Bacon said of children: 'They sweeten labours, but they make misfortunes more bitter.' There is evidence that marriages are likely to be undergoing greater strain at this juncture than at any time since the initial impact of the intimacy of living together. This is not to say the relationship is necessarily poor or in decline; but there may be marital stresses arising from a variety of causes. It is no joke coping with turbulent youngsters if a parent is not getting full support from his or her partner. Difficulties in the marriage may become more exposed, more abrasive, if offspring are rebelling, getting into serious trouble or playing one parent off against the other.

This age group has been referred to as the 'middle generation' because their own parents are usually alive, and they are likely to feel obligations to the younger generation *and* the older one. Some parents feel trapped by the needs of ageing parents and demanding teenagers and wonder whether their own chances of self-realization and self-actualization have vanished.

Unlike their offspring, they are expected to cope, to be patient and strong, and to have no problems and no needs. It is poignant to realize that when older adolescents are searching for meanings – the meaning of life, the meaning and value of self – their parents may be doing something rather similar, though from a different perspective: a kind of evaluation of life and ambitions, fulfilled or unfulfilled. Certainly there are problems – as there are with each transitional stage of development – but there are many compensating sources of satisfaction. For very many parents whose teenagers are approaching independence, or partial independence, there is a sense of freedom and of dawning opportunities to see to oneself again.

Psychologists and psychiatrists have shown an increasing interest in the themes of change, loss and gain which feature in any major period of transition during our lifetime. C. Murray Parkes, a British psychiatrist, describes transitional events as follows:

> In the ongoing flux of life, [the person] undergoes many changes. Arriving, departing, growing, declining, achieving, failing – every change involves a loss and a gain. The old environment must be given up, the new accepted. People come and go; one job is lost, another begun; ... new skills are learnt, old abandoned; expectations are fulfilled or hopes dashed – in all these situations the individual is faced with the need to give up one mode of life and accept another.

Whether the transition is an adolescent change or a mid-life crisis, new behaviours – different responses to changing circumstances – are required. However, young people may undergo a transitional experience without appreciating the nuances of the discontinuity, or without recognizing that a new repertoire of behaviours is called for.

For example, a boy who has prided himself on joining in all the adventures and even occasional lawbreaking with his friends, when urged to try a marijuana joint, may not know how to say no if he is unwilling, how to draw a line under social pressure. A girl may not register any concern about her sexual maturity following her menarche, until she becomes

Reproduced by permission of *Punch*

aware of the implications – when her boyfriend asks her to sleep with him. She must add to an equation, which contains on one side her moral scruples and on the other her own sexual inclinations, the distinct risk of getting pregnant.

This is where an understanding of typical reactions to major transitional events will help parents to follow and guide adolescents in their efforts to cope with the changes in their lives. Dr Barrie Hopson (in his 1986 study) identified the main stages in the fairly predictable sequence of adolescent reactions.

1 *Immobilization.* The youngster has a sense of being overwhelmed, being unable to make plans, to understand or to reason; a kind of paralysis sets in.

2 *Minimization.* He or she may cope with this state of 'deep freeze' by minimizing the changes. The boy affects not to notice the acne of puberty. The disruption and pain caused by the girl's periods are made light of. The youngster may try to trivialize the changes of adolescence. ('I don't know why

everyone makes such a fuss over nothing.') Some will deny that a change has occurred.

3 *Depression*. This is a common feature of adolescence. The physical changes of puberty represent a dramatic transition for the child, and there may be an upsurge in feelings of misery and inner turmoil. Adolescents are quite likely to give vent to self-critical comments. In some cases this leads to more serious moods of depression.

4 *Letting go*. This is the stage of accepting reality for what it is, of figuratively 'letting go' of the past, which means the safety of childhood, of total parental nurturance, of childlike irresponsibility. As Hopson puts it, the person is saying, 'Well, here I am now; here is what I have; I know I can survive; I may not be sure of what I want yet but I will be OK; there is life out there waiting for me.'

5 *Testing*. The 'letting go' provides a bridge to the phase in which young people may begin testing themselves *vis-à-vis* the new circumstances – trying out new behaviours, skills and even (to the anxiety of parents) new and sometimes eccentric lifestyles. At this time quite a lot of anger and irritability can be expressed, so watch out for flak and try to be tolerant.

6 *Search for meaning*. Following this surge of activity and self-testing, there is a more gradual movement towards a search for meaning and understanding of how things are different, and why this is so.

7 *Internalization.* Eventually these new meanings are internalized, and taken into the 'psyche' and behavioural repertoire of the young adult.

Do remember that all transitions involve some stress, sometimes more for particular individuals than others – for example, those who are shy and terrified when faced with a new challenge. Transitions are most distressing if they are unpredictable, involuntary, unfamiliar and of high intensity and magnitude – that is, if the rate and degree of changes are excessive. Parents can help their sons and daughters by warning them of the likely changes, or interpreting them, thus making them more predictable and manageable. Of course, being able to talk about personal and intimate matters to teenagers will depend upon a relationship of trust and good communication, fostered in earlier years.

Often there is no intention to appear to be rejecting the adolescent; repudiations – such as not listening to or fobbing off the child – can occur simply because parents are too busy with other chores, or are tired and irritable after a day's work, and so forth. When such things are part of the *regular pattern* of a teenager's life they are hurtful and damaging. They can arise simply from an insensitivity to adolescent curiosity, maturing intelligence and acute feelings. However, even the most excellent preparation may not be a guarantee against your children distancing themselves from you for a while. Don't let this social withdrawal deter you from taking advantage of the 'right' moment to talk to your son or daughter about the subjects of their distress *and* their joys.

Warm support offered to young people at times of stress goes a long way to reducing its impact on them. Nevertheless, you are likely to be asked why they have to go through such miseries and self-doubt. I personally like Barrie Hopson's answer:

> A transition simultaneously carries the seeds of our yesteryears, the hopes and fears of our futures, and the pressing sensations of the present which is our confirmation of being alive. There is danger and opportunity, ecstasy and despair, development and stagnation, but above all there is movement. Nothing and no-one stays the same. Nature abhors vacuums and stability. A stable state is merely a stopping point on a journey from one place to another. Stop too long and your journey is ended. Stay and enjoy but with the realization that more is to come. You may not be able to stop the journey, but you can fly.

Emotional disorders

Contrary to many parents' fears, adolescence, while certainly not immune from its share of pain for those growing up (and for those guiding the growing-up processes), is not usually characterized by severe emotional disturbance. Nevertheless during the teenage years some 10–15 per cent of adolescents *do* experience significant psychological problems. A sizeable proportion of parents will need to help their children themselves, and if the problems show no signs of being alleviated they should seek expert guidance (see appendix). Although there may be problems, their overall significance and extensiveness have been exaggerated. Psychiatric conditions are probably a little commoner during adolescence than during middle childhood, but the difference is not very great, and most adolescents do *not* manifest psychiatric disorders.

All sorts of terms (or euphemisms) have been used to refer to the more troublesome psychological problems displayed by children and teenagers. There is the popular and ubiquitous expression 'maladjusted' and other designations such as 'nervous', 'highly strung', 'emotionally disturbed', 'difficult', to mention but a few. They refer collectively to a large and mixed bag of disorders ranging from depression, anxiety, inhibition and shyness to non-compliance, destructiveness, stealing and aggression. In essence, these problems represent exaggerations, deficits (deficiencies) or disabling combinations of feelings, attitudes and behaviours common, at one time or the other, to most young people. Aggression, shyness, and a combination of low self-esteem and poor concentration are examples of each category.

There is a distinction between those difficulties which primarily lead to emotional disturbance or distress for the young people themselves (e.g. anxiety, shyness, depression, feelings of inferiority and timidity) and those which mainly involve the kinds of antisocial behaviour (e.g. aggression, lying, stealing and disobedience) which disrupt the wellbeing of others, notably those in frequent contact with the young person (see chapter 4).

The first category, referred to by psychologists as 'emotional disorders', are manifested by about 2½ per cent of pre-adolescent children. Their prevalence increases somewhat by adolescence, and we find that boys and girls are about equally prone to them. For most children these kinds of problems manifest themselves briefly at certain periods and then become minimal or disappear completely.

We know as a result of longitudinal studies (which follow up people from infancy to adulthood) that, for the most part, young people who suffer from emotional disorders become reasonably well-adjusted adults. In a sense these difficulties are the emotional equivalent of 'growing pains'. They come and go; nevertheless they sometimes persist, and can reach levels of intensity which cause all-round suffering.

This is all very well, but you might well wish to know whether there are any *typical* adolescent problems, typical in the sense that they reflect stresses and strains which differ from those emerging in childhood or, indeed, adult life. There certainly are serious but relatively rare psychiatric disorders, such as schizophrenia and anorexia or bulimia nervosa, whose onset is particularly associated with the teenage years. (This book is not primarily concerned with relatively rare conditions like schizophrenia, although you will find a note about it and psychiatric treatment, in the appendix). However, at the level of developmental problems, we can witness in the transition from childhood to adulthood an upsurge of moodiness and feelings of misery. Adolescents are often tormented by low self-esteem, worries about the future, and fears about such matters as attending school or participating in social activities.

You can rest assured that, although the rates of feelings of unhappiness and self-depreciation reach a peak during adolescence, the *majority* of teenagers seem generally to be happy and confident and are not the victims of serious depression or of other emotional disturbance. In fact, adolescence does not quite live up to its reputation. This may reassure those of you who are bracing yourselves with trepidation for your child's entry into adolescence, but it is cold comfort for those for whom this is only a statistical generalization. The 10–15 per cent of young people who do experience significant psychological problems certainly find adolescence an ordeal; and the parents – feeling like barometers registering adolescent squalls, not to mention storms – might well cry out for help.

At what point is it inappropriate to be philosophical about your teenager's difficulties? When should your mental alarm bells begin to ring; when do you cease saying, 'Ah well, she'll grow out of it?' At the most general level you might ask yourself:

1 What are the consequences – benign or unfavourable – of her actions?
2 Does her behaviour prevent her from leading a contented life in which she is able to enjoy social relationships, and play and work (learn) effectively?

Your answers to these very broad questions could be important, because problem behaviours have unfavourable consequences for adolescents and/or those in contact with them. Generally speaking there is an association between intense and prolonged feelings of unhappiness and psychological disorder; there is a loss of a sense of wellbeing.

There are more specific questions to ask. Affirmative answers to several of the following questions might well be of significance:

1 Does my child get excessively miserable, embarrassed, shy, hostile, anxious or morbidly guilty?
2 Does she give vent to anger too easily?
3 Is her tolerance of frustration low?
4 Is she inflexible in the face of failure?
5 Does she find it difficult to cope with novel or difficult situations?
6 Does she experience difficulty in establishing affectionate, lasting relationships with adults and peers?
7 Does she fail to learn from experience or from disciplinary situations?

8 Does she not get on with teachers or other adults in
  authority?

Depression and suicide

As the realities of the new responsibilities of young adulthood
and the difficulties of sexual adjustment become unmistak-
able, the usual feelings of misery and inner turmoil give way,
in some adolescents, to more serious moods of depression – a
sense of helplessness and powerlessness, of events being out
of or beyond control. Some teenagers even entertain ideas
about committing suicide.

The milder form of depression may show itself as a lack of
physical energy and wellbeing. In its more severe manifestations, adolescents tend to be irritable and bad-tempered,
and, when it is at its worst, they sleep poorly, lack an
appetite, and are always dejected, apathetic and lifeless.
Teenagers who are (for whatever reason) depressed feel
helpless, sad and useless and find it sometimes impossible to
meet the challenges of life. They cease to strive and to use
their full effectiveness in whatever sphere of activity they find
themselves.

The apathy of a young person with poor health is often
mistaken for laziness. If a child is to be successful at school,
good health is vital; it provides the basis for the stamina
demanded by hours of concentration in the classroom.
Regular attendance at school depends upon it, and effective
learning, in turn, depends upon reasonably consistent presence
at lessons.

The checklist below may help you to detect signs of
depression in your son or daughter:

1 a demeanour of unhappiness and misery (more persistent
  and intense than 'the blues' which we all suffer from now
  and then);
2 a marked change in eating and/or sleeping patterns;
3 a feeling of helplessness, hopelessness and self-dislike;
4 an inability to concentrate and apply oneself to anything;

5 everything (even talking and dressing) seen as an effort;
6 irritating or aggressive behaviour;
7 a sudden change in school work;
8 a constant search for distractions and new activities;
9 dangerous risk-taking (e.g. with drugs/alcohol; dangerous driving; delinquent actions);
10 friends being dropped or ignored.

Depression can be masked in adolescence and thus not easily detected. Another problem for the alert parent is that any item in the list above *can occur normally* in adolescence without in any way indicating a depressive disorder. So what is one to do? The questions below will help you to judge whether to seek professional advice if your answers tend to be in the affirmative.

1 Are there several of the signs (listed above) present in your teenager?
2 Do they occur frequently?
3 Have they persisted for a long time?
4 Do they cause *extensive* suffering to him/her?
5 Do they stand in the way of his/her development towards maturity?
6 Do they get in the way of his/her relationships with (a) peers, (b) adults?
7 Do they cause distress in others?

It seems paradoxical that the high standards which many pre-adolescents and adolescents set themselves also create problems for them. All the evidence indicates that young people who are highly self-critical, those for whom there is a large discrepancy between the way they actually see themselves and the way they would ideally like to be, tend to be anxious, insecure, depressed and somewhat cynical. Sometimes they lapse into feelings of despair.

Depression is a common feature of suicide, which, in adolescents, is usually associated with emotional and behavioural problems related to psychological and social stress. Suicide rates rise sharply during the teens so that it comes to rank among the half-dozen most common causes of death among older adolescents. (The figures are still well below those for adults, and only a minute fraction of the suicide rate in old age.)

Attempted suicide is very much a late adolescent phenomenon, the peak being among 15–19-year-olds. There has been a tenfold increase in such incidents since the 1960s among adolescent boys and a fivefold rise for girls. Nevertheless the rate of attempted suicides for adolescent girls far exceeds that for boys. No one seems able to explain the surge in the statistics. It does not seem to be related to drug abuse or to too liberal prescribing of tablets by doctors. It may be associated with increased use of alcohol, and it is most likely linked in some way with the increasing prevalence of marital discord, childhood separations, unemployment and criminality.

Teenagers sometimes have fantasies about their death which involve their 'ending it all' and yet surviving the event by 'attending' their own funeral where they are able to savour the grief and guilt displayed by errant parents or boyfriends/girlfriends. These fantasies indicate how, in some adolescents, the finality of death is not fully appreciated, or at least not while in a depressed or hysterical state, and not at the time when the gesture (and, often, more than a gesture) of suicide is contemplated. The cliché that suicide is often a cry for help is true despite its banality. Threats of suicide should not be treated lightly and not dismissed with the words 'If she really meant it she would do it, not threaten to do it.' Many individuals who have threatened to commit suicide do in the end carry out their threat. In cases of adolescent depression and/or suicide you should consult your doctor as a means to a referral to a clinical psychologist or psychiatrist.

Abnormal fears: phobias and anxiety

A modicum of fear can help to prepare a youngster to cope with testing situations (examinations, athletic contests) which require peak efficiency. Beyond a certain level of intensity it can be debilitating and even 'paralysing', as with some able teenagers who cannot cope with written exams and fail despite their good class record.

An analysis of children's fears at various ages suggests that certain situations tend to evoke worries at particular phases of development. Older children and adolescents tend to fear intangible things and have fears about social situations. Children of 11 and 12 admit more fear of the occult, of the dark, of strange and unfamiliar places and people, of being alone, of strange noises, lights, shadows, of deformed and mutilated people, of nightmares and night apparitions than young children. Older children also admit more fears of being scolded or embarrassed or of not doing the right thing. Studies of the fears of childhood and early adolescence indicate that they are so common that it might be said to be 'normal' to be fearful about one thing or another, at different stages in their development.

At the age of 11, children exhibit an increase in fear. Among 11- and 12-year-olds, worries connected with school are nearly half as many again as worries about home matters. In Britain, 11 is that awkward age in a youngster's life when the change from junior to senior school is being made. It may not be coincidental that it is also the age at which phobias about school are at a high peak. Abnormal fears (phobias) involve an intense dread in the presence of an object or situation often amounting to panic and, although the object may be individual to the adolescent, certain forms are common, for example dread of open or closed spaces, height, water, and so on. Some definitions of phobia emphasize the incapacitating or restrictive effect of a phobia, in contrast to the more common fears which most of us endure.

There are various types of phobia. For example, some teenagers have a persistent fear of, and compelling desire to avoid, a social situation (say, a party) in which they are exposed to possible scrutiny by others and fear that they may act in a manner that will cause embarrassment or humiliation. In the case of agoraphobia, the youngster has an intense fear of, and thus avoids, being alone or in public places from which escape might be difficult or help not available in the case of sudden incapacitation – such as packed supermarkets, public transport, bridges, tunnels, lifts. The sufferer knows that he or she has unreasonable fears and doesn't welcome being told the obvious. After all, panic is beyond voluntary control. Nor can it be explained or reasoned away, as well-intentioned parents hope and insist.

A phobia has four components: the psychological, the physical (or physiological), the behavioural and the social. The *psychological* component is anxiety. Phobic adolescents tend to display two types of anxiety, *general* fear and *situational* (or anticipatory) fear, that is the kind that is aroused as they approach the feared object.

Phobic individuals experience a variety of *physiological* responses on exposure to the feared object or situation – tachycardia (palpitations), increased perspiration, increased respiratory rate and uneasy feelings in the abdomen. Sometimes these feelings are so severe they amount to panic and the sufferer may even faint.

The *behavioural* component – avoidance – is central to the phobic teenager's problem. It may be necessary to go to all sorts of extremes to 'avoid' exposure to the feared object or situation. The behavioural problem provokes in turn a *social* one. The need to 'avoid' causes interference in the ability to lead a normal life. The degree of interference very much depends upon the phobic object or situation. If it is commonplace, interference may be considerable. It may be so severe that individuals are unable to work or to leave the security of their own homes. Not only are their own lives disturbed but so are the lives of others, often deliberately manipulated.

Fear and anxiety wreak their havoc, not only in such psychological manifestations as dread, apprehension and tension, but also in the form of physical illness. The term 'stress syndrome' is often used to describe any state of emotional overload where the human being has been pushed to his or her limits. Individuals differ markedly in their reactions to 'difficult' situations. For example, examinations may be stressful for some pupils but not for others. An understanding of what is stressful for a particular youngster always requires careful analysis of the particular settings and circumstances in which they occur, and the individual's reaction to them.

Whether stresses are immediate and extreme, or whether they are chronic and seemingly petty threats, frustrations and conflicts of modern life, they erode the young person's emotional and physical wellbeing in much the same way. Perhaps the major physical stresses that people have to face today are overcrowding and noise (although there seems to be an exception for young people when it comes to music). We know that, in both animals and humans, these irritations produce psychological and physiological effects, including aggression, anxiety and fear. So do the psychological stresses inherent in a highly competitive and success-orientated society.

The changes in behaviour which people go through under stress are also matched by changes in the body. Victims of stress may go to their physicians to be treated for disorders that do not always appear to have any physical origin – the so-called psychosomatic disorders. Medical treatment can alleviate the symptoms for a time, but they are likely to return when the patient is again confronted with a stressful situation.

Methods found most effective in helping young people to overcome fears include:

1 helping them to develop skills by which they can cope with the feared object or situation;
2 taking them by degrees into active contact and participation with the feared object or situation;
3 giving them an opportunity gradually to become acquainted with the feared object or situation under circumstances that at the same time give them the opportunity either to inspect or to ignore it.

Methods that are sometimes helpful in enabling an individual to overcome fears include:

1 verbal explanation and reassurance;
2 verbal explanation plus a practical demonstration that the feared object or situation is not dangerous;
3 giving the person examples of fearlessness regarding the feared object or situation (parents frequently quote the example of other young people who are not afraid);
4 conditioning the youngster to believe that the feared object is not dangerous but pleasurable or, at least, neutral.

It has been found that, even without help, children and teenagers can overcome fears, by using the following techniques:

1 they could practise overcoming their fear by enlisting the help of adults;
2 they could talk with other people about the things they fear;
3 they could argue with themselves about the reality or unreality of the dreaded imaginary creatures or fantasized events – say, death – that they fear.

School refusal

School phobias – more aptly named school refusal – illustrate neatly the psychosomatic ramifications of adolescent fear. The young person who is desperately afraid of some aspect of attending school has recurrent physical symptoms for which no adequate cause can be found, and these, again, are inclined to be changeable.

The school refusal crisis, well under way, is apt to affect the entire family; and the breakfast scene (on school days) is likely to be harrowing. Parents display varying degrees of anxiety, anger or despairing resignation. If adolescents are being cajoled or pressured to go to school, they are likely to present physical signs of intense distress. They may be pale and tremulous; they may have a frequent need to urinate, or they may suffer from diarrhoea. They usually complain of physical malaise and a variety of ailments, most particularly abdominal pains and headache. They are likely to be off their food – particularly breakfast – and to feel nauseous and perhaps have bouts of vomiting. Obviously the parents must have the physical complaints checked by the doctor, but these generally prove to have no organic basis. They are inclined to subside at weekends and during school holidays or, even, shortly after the parents have resigned themselves to keeping the youngster at home.

The onset of school refusal is usually rather gradual; a build-up of tension, in the form of irritability, restlessness, disturbed sleep, vomiting and abdominal pain precede the full manifestation of the problem. And from the youngster's initial attitude of unwillingness, hedged around by varying excuses and complaints, the problem escalates to an outright refusal to set out for school.

School refusal tends to follow, not infrequently, a legitimate absence from school. Some subjects (e.g. mathematics, arithmetic) are hierarchical in structure; that is, one step is logically preceded by, and dependent upon, another. So the adolescent who misses a series of lessons (particularly if he or she has chronic recurrent illnesses) may find it very difficult to catch up. Subjects like these, which tend anyway to attract negative emotional attitudes, may (in the absence of an understanding teacher) become the focus of intense anxiety for the vulnerable child.

In chapter 8, I explain how to distinguish between school refusal and truancy. But when a teenager has symptoms like those described above it is best to consult the head of school very early on.

Now let us look at a case of an intense fear of going to school. Mark, a 12-year-old boy, with a hypersensitive, timid personality, was dealt with harshly by a teacher during a maths lesson. The fortuitous association of subject-matter and classroom with the humiliating and frightening experience appeared to make him feel anxious not only during maths lessons but even when entering the classroom in the absence of the maths teacher. The anxiety soon generalized further so that he felt anxious when he approached the school, let alone the classroom. Nevertheless, he had to make the effort to approach the classroom. But he began to feel panicky. Avoidance of the area led to relief from anxiety.

In this way – it is thought – the habit of avoidance had become reinforced. The attachment of fear to the previously unfeared classroom is thought to proceed on the basis of classical conditioning (see chapter 10). The sheer relief of escaping from a distressing situation (school) and being at home, safe with his mother, constituted an additional pay-off for Mark's school refusal.

The anxiety, conditioned as it is to various stimuli but not under conscious control, comes into action despite the adolescent's best efforts to combat it. The dread of school can be of such intensity that those who are still trying unsuccessfully to get their children to school find that they are obdurate in the face of entreaties, recriminations and punishment. Not even weighty authority, in the person of the headteacher, will budge them.

Parents' anxieties are threefold: concern at their children's palpable unhappiness and at their impotence to alleviate their apparent dread of school; worries about the effect of prolonged absence on their school work (an important consideration in a competitive educational system); and apprehension over their legal responsibility to ensure their children's attendance at school.

Fortunately some resourceful parents have devised their own methods of dealing with their offsprings' fears and anxieties. However, a point may be reached – as with Mark's severe phobic anxiety – when it is best to seek professional assistance.

Behavioural methods have provided the cornerstone of treatment for phobias. The aims of treatment are fourfold:

1 to reduce levels of both general and situational anxiety;
2 to relieve disturbing physiological symptoms;
3 to reduce avoidance behaviour;
4 to prevent interference in daily living.

The fearful youngster may be exposed to the phobic object or situation in fantasy, in pictures or in real life. Exposure may be graded, by means of a hierarchical challenge programme (described below) or given all at once. Self-exposure home-work, in which children are given a graded series of tasks to perform and progressively record their anxiety levels on some simple rating scale, has been found very effective.

Let us look at the work of a clinical psychologist who used behaviour therapy (and the method called 'exposure training') to reintroduce Mark into school on a gradual basis. This approach avoids the dangers of further delays due to his refusal to go. Mark was taught how to relax, and the tactics were carefully explained. He and his therapist would go to the school early in the morning when no one else was present. Mark was asked to report any feelings of rising tension. As soon as he did so the therapist immediately took Mark back to the car and praised him for what he had achieved so far. The therapist and the boy approached the school together in a series of steps graded from the least anxiety-provoking situation (sitting in a car in front of the school) to the most anxiety-provoking condition (being in the classroom with the teacher and other pupils present). At the end of a three-day period of what is also called desensitization, Mark was able to stay in the library all morning doing set work. Next, he managed to stay a full school day. After this achievement, he could come to school unaccompanied. In the next week (following careful preparation) he sat in with the class for his best subject, English. Week by week more lessons (maths, finally) were built into his timetable, so that it was not long before Mark had returned to school com-pletely.

The presence of the therapist (with whom he had a good relationship) was considered as a strong positive stimulus evoking a *relaxed* emotional response. The graduated re-entry into school life was so designed that Mark's confidence in the therapist would counteract fears aroused by each new step forward in the treatment programme.

Co-operation of parents and school is, of course, of great importance. The type of individual therapy programme to be instituted will be determined by the exact nature of the child's disturbance. As with other emotional disorders of childhood, the long-term prognosis for school refusers is generally good. But some school refusers who have been untreated, or inadequately treated, have become work refusers in adolescence or adulthood.

Anorexia nervosa

A problem particularly associated with adolescent girls (it *can* also occur in pre-pubertal children) is anorexia nervosa. The anorexic girl deliberately restricts her food intake; indeed, she does not want to eat at all, because she believes she is fat and wishes to lose weight. Most people today have heard of this once esoteric disorder. The word 'anorexia' means loss of appetite. However, the absence of hunger or appetite is *not* a crucial feature of anorexia nervosa. Nevertheless, the teenager will characteristically act as if she had lost her appetite.

Anorexia nervosa is essentially about weight rather than eating. The really central feature of the disorder is a body weight which is abnormally low for the age, height and sex of the person. There is a further crucial feature: the individual's attitude to her weight. What makes life difficult for parents and other would-be helpers is that someone with anorexia nervosa will not always be open or truthful about her feelings. If she is, she will say that she is ashamed and very frightened of the thoughts of being heavier. She may suffer in various ways through being thin, but compared with putting on weight it is seen as the lesser evil.

This is how a late adolescent client described herself to me:

When I try to see myself as I am, I see an obese, not very attractive girl. I drink too much and as my ultimate aim is not to eat at all, I am a dismal failure. At one time if I drank I wouldn't eat but now I drink too much, lose control and binge which is disgusting. I think bingeing is the most degrading thing anyone can do and drinking is a close second so in my eyes I am a very lowly person.

You will have noticed that this young woman mentions bingeing. There is in fact a variation in symptomatology called bulimia nervosa in which the individual has binges – rather joyless, guilt-ridden episodes of excessive eating – followed by self-induced vomiting and the abuse of laxatives. My client, like many other anorexics, had at one time ceased to menstruate – a sign of disordered physiology brought about by her severe dieting.

Slimming is an obsession in our culture today. People (women in particular) are bombarded with propaganda based upon the achievement of health and beauty. Being overweight is stigmatized, and the condition is viewed both as a physical deformity and as a behavioural aberration. Many fat people are chastised for their lack of self-control and held responsible for their voluntary, self-inflicted disability. Many mortified and ashamed fat people, full of self-disparagement and self-hatred, are further disadvantaged because they are not only discriminated against but are made to feel that they deserve such discrimination. Because they come to accept their treatment as just, a self-fulfilling prophecy develops, since the way we imagine ourselves to appear to another person is an essential element in our conception of ourselves. Self-fulfilling prophecies come true because the characteristics presented become part of the victims' picture of themselves; fat people who are repeatedly told that they are endangering their health are being told, in effect, 'We expect you to be sick.' Eventually the role of sick person becomes second nature to them. Similarly, the disturbed fat person who is told by the society that he or she is inferior may begin to condemn himself or herself and experience a disturbed body image.

The main feature of disturbance of the body image in obesity is a preoccupation with obesity, often to the exclusion of any other personal characteristic. It may make no difference whether the person is talented, wealthy or intelligent; weight is his or her overriding concern, and he or she sees the world in terms of body weight.

One often repeated explanation for stigmatizing overweight

people is that, in a society which has historically been suffused with a Protestant ethic, one characteristic of which is a strong emphasis on impulse control, fatness suggests a kind of immorality that invites retribution. Correspondingly, not being overweight and avoiding the contagion of gluttony implies self-denial, which ought to bring appropriate rewards, including good health.

There may be another 'bonus' in being trim; the sexual motive also pervades advertising on slimming preparations and regimes. If slimming is normal (i.e. usual or common) among people and especially young women, why does the anorexic 'go over the top'? The truth is that anorexia nervosa remains a mystery to us. The anorexic who appears so pathetically (and sometimes grotesquely) thin and emaciated is quite likely to misperceive her appearance. What for her is slender or fat, what is a normal *weight* for her height and age, or what is an attractive *shape*, is quite at odds with the judgement of most other people.

Psychoanalytic writers place great emphasis on the relationship between feeding (early oral gratification) and the evolving sense of self and the perception of others' attitudes and expectations. The acts of eating and fasting are loaded with meanings – personal, familial, cultural and religious. They also carry the connotations of control and self-mastery, of nurturant love, comfort, sociability and, indeed, sexuality. The 'meaning' of the eating disorder for one anorexic teenager is likely to differ at certain points when compared with another. Each must be individually assessed by professionals.

There is evidence that families of anorexics place greater than average stress upon food and eating. They may unwittingly reinforce or initiate tendencies in the make-up of the youngster which give peculiar importance and meaning to food, the act of eating, and the image of her self and body.

There are different patterns of causation, rather than one fixed path to anorexia nervosa. Parents need to be alert to signs in their teenager of incipient anorexia nervosa: a preoccupation, indeed obsession, with calorie counts, with having 'a say' (control) over her diet, loss of weight, cessation of periods, concern over appearance, moodiness, and so on. It would be advisable to seek professional advice early rather than late, if the alarm bells in your head begin sounding.

Chapter Four

Defiance: antisocial and criminal behaviour

The older generation, showing a convenient amnesia for what *its* parents said, looks askance at the 'lack' of discipline, obedience and respect among the young, most especially among adolescents. The reasons are not hard to find. Compliance to rules – whether they are laid down by convention, in laws, or hidden away in our consciences – is fundamental to social living. All parents and teachers are beset at one time or another by disobedient and rebellious teenagers, and usually they try to be tolerant. But there are different degrees of rebellion. Parents and teachers are more sensitive to 'revolts' against certain kinds of rules than others.

Flouting society: crime and violence

There are children and teenagers whose behaviour is notable for their fundamental inability or unwillingness to adhere to the rules and codes of conduct prescribed by society at its various levels: family, school and, indeed, the community at large. It is when adolescents break those rules that might be called 'moral rules' that parents get most perturbed. Conduct problems cover a lot of territory, including as they do seriously antisocial acts as well as what is only moderately troublesome behaviour. Although conduct problems can create misery for everyone concerned with the younger child, the disturbance can often be contained within the home or classroom – although often at great cost.

As children grow older those problems that involve a

persistent defiance of authority, together with a refusal or inability to show self-restraint, become more serious in their implications. They extend more and more beyond the confines of the child's life at home and school. The reverberations of the child's misdemeanours may eventually lead to the danger not only of being labelled 'conduct-disordered', but also of earning the designation 'juvenile delinquent' if he or she infringes the law, is apprehended and found guilty. It is clear from self-reports of delinquent-type behaviour that large numbers of young people engage in delinquent acts for several years before they receive a police caution or are found guilty of offences.

The number of young people committing detected and adjudicated crimes in the United Kingdom and the United States has increased markedly. What was once an almost completely male preserve now includes substantial numbers of female offenders. The average age for the first court appearance of juveniles is lower, and there is a marked trend towards more violent offences.

The term 'juvenile delinquent' is merely an administrative term, not a clinical diagnosis. It has to be recognized that relatively minor delinquent activities (e.g. petty thefts, vandalism) are surprisingly common in the teens. Such activities tend to be transitory. However, there is a small but hard core of adolescents who habitually break the law. Delinquency is perhaps the most noteworthy of all activities as an adolescent manifestation, reaching a peak at 15 years for boys and 14 years for girls. By their twenties most of the former offenders have gradually become broadly law-abiding members of the community. But there is nothing to be complacent about.

To take one delinquent activity as an illustration, theft is a transient adolescent phenomenon involving large numbers of young people. An important 1975 survey of 1425 London boys, by the psychologist W. Belson, showed that 88 per cent had at some time stolen something from school, and 70 per cent from a shop. By no means were all the thefts trivial, and not all theft will prove to be a transitory phenomenon. The more serious antisocial acts begin relatively early in life. Almost 60 per cent of teenage delinquents committed their first offence (although it may not have been detected then) *before* the child's tenth birthday, and the early onset applies to theft in particular. Among the factors which may break this longer-term pattern before it is too late are firm supervision and early detection of the misdemeanour by the police.

The transition from completely demanding babyhood to the demand-obeying status of older children insisted on by parents – often in the second and third years of life – can be marked by confrontations and noisy temper tantrums. Displays of oppositional, aggressive and other forms of coercive behaviour are common in toddlers and older children. In the setting of a reasonably robust family, such outbursts are coped with by most parents. Parents differ in their methods. By adolescence, boys and girls have been trained socially (socialized), and are expected to be able to control their tempers and aggressive outbursts most of the time. Yet one can observe in some teenagers a resurgence of the outbursts of early childhood.

Even as adults, we lose our 'cool' and lash out verbally at times. The point is that anger and aggression are 'normal' reactions to frustration in young children; anger in young and older adults is also normal, but giving vent to it in frequent or intense outbursts of verbal aggression or physical violence is certainly not. Such behaviour might involve destructiveness, hooliganism, assault and disruptive actions.

Hooliganism and vandalism among young people are topics seldom out of the newspapers. (However, a search through newspaper archives reveals that hooliganism and troublemaking among youths was always a concern of their elders.) There are various categories of vandalism. The most persistent form of wanton and arbitrary destruction is carried out by teenagers who feel they are 'outsiders', and who lash out at society out of resentment and frustration. Much of their behaviour is motivated by a search for status among their peers. For most youngsters over 16 years this need is becoming less pressing. Most other boys of their age are now spending more time with girlfriends, or are already married, or have a job. The outsider feels inadequate by comparison. This sort of person is more likely than other vandals to commit offences of other kinds, especially burglary or theft.

Pressures by the peer group play a large part in the acts of vandalism in the 13–16 age group. Acts of daring and competition leave a trail of broken park benches, windows and road signs. Many of the adolescents at this stage (it is usually transient) indulge in other types of delinquency, such as shoplifting and gang fights.

Causes of antisocial behaviour

Teenagers have to be taught that, however uncongenial and difficult social and moral rules may be to keep, we cannot contract out. Moral rules, in particular, are foundational in the sense that they are concerned with the maintenance of trust, mutual help and justice in human relationships. Unless adolescents have acquired some respect for these kinds of attribute, it becomes virtually impossible for them to be integrated into meaningful social life. Moral rules form the yardstick against which we evaluate the rules of any particular social activity.

It is not surprising that, though conventions and customs vary widely from one society to another, a number of basic moral principles apparently do not. It is necessary to look more closely at moral conformity if we are to understand its failures. Despite the general tendency of socialization to produce a degree of uniformity of behaviour among the members of a society, idiosyncrasies, failures and distortions of socialization and character, obviously occur. Such idiosyncrasies sometimes produce brilliant and creative individualists. Indeed, Western society pays lip-service (if not a genuine reverence) to individualism; and socialization is meant to leave space for individual character development. The out-and-out failure of social training may produce citizens who are poorly adapted to their society. These are the undersocialized, nonconforming, sometimes conscienceless young people who are delinquent or even psychopathic.

Researchers have demonstrated that there are regular changes or stages in a person's conscience, as shown by his or her moral judgements. These stages are related to the young person's level of cognitive (i.e. intellectual) development. Young children, for example, tend to view moral questions in terms of physical consequences to the self, basically an egoistic view of the world. Conventional thinking, a later development, characterizes most people; it places moral issues in the context of conventional rules, such as commonly held codes of behaviour, religious precepts or the laws of society. Principled moral judgements are at the most abstract level in the developmental progression. They involve universal human values such as justice and reciprocity, considered within a system of higher good, and transcending the laws or rules of any one particular group.

It is not until adolescence that the individual has the intellectual capacity to achieve this level of moral awareness, but that of itself is not sufficient to give the teenager a form of principled morality. Until adolescents have a commitment to an identity, including a consistent ideology, true principled moral judgement is not possible. For those interested in behaviour in a moral sense, this is an intriguing theory, raising such questions as 'Has the perpetrator of violent crime only managed to develop a commitment to ideology at a low level in the scheme of moral judgement?' Certainly many delinquent youths function at a pre-conventional level.

It is important to remember that persistent flouting of codes and conventions in the seriously disturbed adolescent is not only related to frequent lapses of poorly established controls or to the failure to learn these controls in the first place. There is also the possibility that the behavioural and moral standards that a child has absorbed in the family or neighbourhood do not coincide with the norms of society in general.

If members of a society conform, then they must conform to something. The term 'norm' is used to describe the collective expectation of how one should behave. Any organized society, whether primitive or complex, has its norms, and deals with deviation from these norms in different ways. In any community consisting of many individuals, the absence of a stable framework of rules and standards or a faulty method of induction into the social system would lead to anarchy. The sociologist Patricia Morgan (in her 1978 study) paints a sombre picture of a growing number of poorly socialized individuals – adolescents and adults – who have scarcely acquired the rudiments of human culture. As she puts it:

> much crime, often of a highly dangerous and serious nature, is committed by those well under the age of criminal responsibility. . . . Actually, to use the expression 'crime' for much modern anti-social behaviour is rather misleading, since it has no end beyond the most transitory titillation. The delinquent is frequently far too unsocialized to control his pursuit of instant excitement for rational gain.

It is worth knowing about the Gluecks' 1968 study. Sheldon and Eleanor Glueck carefully matched 500 delinquent boys with an equal number of boys not identified as delinquent. The boys were matched for residence in underprivileged areas, age, ethnic origin, family size and overall tested intelligence. These 1000 boys had spent their early years in underprivileged areas of Boston, Massachusetts. The boys averaged 14 years of age when first taken into the study. Extensive background studies were conducted in an attempt to find childhood precursors of delinquent careers. Follow-up investigations lasted until the participants were 31 years old, yielding valuable information on adult outcomes of delinquent and non-delinquent careers.

Boys in both the delinquent and non-delinquent groups came from large families, averaging six and five brothers/sisters respectively. However, the researchers found evidence of greater family disorganization among boys with delinquent careers. Other family members exhibited patterns of behaviour such as alcoholism and criminality to a greater degree than did the families of non-delinquent boys. There was more separation and divorce in the delinquent group. The delinquent homes were characterized as having less supervision for the boys and fewer rules, such as set meals and bedtimes. The Gluecks regarded family disorganization as the central precursor of a delinquent career.

They found little evidence for any differences in physical characteristics between the two groups. All the boys were given a series of physical and mental examinations. While it was reported that the delinquents tended to be more sturdily built, the physical examinations revealed no differences in physical health. The delinquent boys had many school problems. Among the delinquent group, 41 per cent were two or more years behind the proper grade, compared to 21 per cent of the non-delinquents. Truancy was also very high among the delinquent boys: 95 per cent were truants, compared to only 10 per cent of the non-delinquents.

What of the outcomes of the two groups in terms of adult criminal behaviour? In adulthood the delinquent boys were arrested for many more criminal offences than their non-delinquent counterparts. While the original 'non-delinquent' group engaged in some official delinquency in their adult years, boys who were official juvenile delinquents showed a decline in criminal behaviour into adulthood. Before the age of 17, 90 per cent of the delinquent boys had committed one or more serious offences. Between the ages of 17 and 25 the percentage of serious offenders had fallen to 60 per cent, and between 25 and 31 it had declined to 29 per cent.

In interviews with the project psychiatrist, the delinquent boys often made negative statements about school, such as: 'I hate school because I am always left behind'; 'It is too hard'; 'I want to go to work'. More boys in the delinquent group did, in fact, drop out of school before the age of 16 than in the non-delinquent group. This is in spite of the fact that the two groups – delinquent and non-delinquent – were matched for overall intelligence.

Perhaps the most striking finding about delinquency was

the degree of delinquency among close friends. Among the delinquent groups, 98 per cent reported having friends who were official delinquents; this compared to only 7 per cent among the non-delinquent group.

'Normal' friends will not have been easy to come by in any group of deviant adolescents. There is a relationship between the young person's status as 'deviant' and the likelihood of being rejected by peers. Parents commonly report that grudging acceptance or outright rejection by other children is a feature of their aggressive and disruptive offsprings' lives. Their interactions with their peers tend to be negative, marked by aversive behaviours (verbal and physical abuse, for example) rather than mutually reinforcing activities.

It is not only in the area of academic skills that deviant young persons show deficits. Their social skills are poorly developed in many instances. Indeed it could be said that much of what we call 'emotional disturbance' is gauche and clumsy social behaviour.

Antisocial children receive more aversive 'input' – negative messages about themselves, more criticism and punishment – than other members of their family. One would expect that at some point they would develop a negative image of themselves and others. Low self-esteem is, as we have seen, a thread running strongly through many psychological problems of adolescence. But many teenagers whose antisocial activities take the form of extreme coercive, aggressive actions come through with their self-esteem intact. They do not assign blame to themselves, nor do they see themselves as less worthy than others. What they acquire over the years is an extremely negative view of their family, their peers and, in time, the police and society itself, together with its value system.

Gerald Patterson, an American clinical psychologist (distinguished for his work with families), is of the opinion that young people at risk of psychological problems have little *feeling of efficacy* in arranging their own lives. Many antisocial youngsters convey a sense of events moving outside of their control, as if they were almost *impelled* to steal that article, or attack that person. And this is dangerously combined with an essentially antisocial *attitude* to others – a self-righteous commitment to violence as a solution to problems. Such people are outsiders to society, and, in their own perception, responsibility is not theirs; they are not to blame.

Patricia Morgan is highly critical of the role of the present-day nuclear family and the vogue for child-centred schemes of childrearing. In her opinion they have proved unequal to the unremitting, painstaking and detailed socialization tasks of producing in children such socially desirable qualities as competence, co-operation, responsibility, and moral awareness and restraint. Sociologists and criminologists would see this viewpoint as far too simple, ignoring as it does social, economic, political and other 'structural' forces operating inexorably on individuals and families to their detriment.

Nevertheless, the available evidence on family influences suggests that children with *persistent* delinquent problems come most often from families notable for their disharmony and quarrelling, for an absence of affection, and for inconsistent discipline which is ineffective and either extremely severe or completely lax. Knowing something of such evidence, caring and loving parents find it a shock (and feel it to be a disgrace) when their son or daughter is reported to them for delinquent activities, and they ask themselves despairingly where they went wrong. It is important to remember that parents are not infallible, nor are they all-powerful. Others also exert an influence – for good or ill – on their offspring.

Social policies and political decisions are of importance in dealing with the wider ramifications of delinquency. Levels of unemployement and poverty, the quality of education and housing, and the feeling of having a stake in society, all play their part in creating the climate for, or reduction of, crime. However, there are personal steps one can take to maximize the child's or teenager's resistance to temptation, in situations of potential danger. These are described in the last section of this chapter.

The problems of adolescent aggression, destructiveness and vandalism have been the subject of extensive psychological research. For example, psychologists consistently find that aggressive youths have parents who tend to favour the use of physical punishment, to disagree with each other, and to be cold and rejecting to their offspring.

Parents of non-aggressive adolescents rarely reinforce their sons for resorting to physical aggression in response to provocation. Aggressive behaviour is penalized. Parents of aggressive teenagers, on the other hand, tolerate no aggressive displays whatsoever in the *home*, but condone, actively encourage and reinforce provocative and aggressive actions towards others in the *community*.

A combination of lax discipline and hostile attitudes on the part of both parents encourages very aggressive and poorly controlled behaviour in their offspring. The pattern of childrearing that produces the most hostile children is one where the parents use punitive methods persistently against a background of rejecting, hostile parental attitudes. These methods are often referred to as power-assertive; the adult asserts dominant and authoritarian control through physical punishment, harsh verbal abuse, angry threats and deprivation of privileges.

It would seem that physical violence is the least effective form of discipline or training when it comes to moulding a child's behaviour. There is a positive relationship between the extensive use of physical punishment in the home by parents and high levels of aggression in their offspring outside the home. All the evidence to date shows that physical methods of punishment (the deliberate infliction of pain on the child) may for the time being suppress the behaviour that it is meant to inhibit, but the long-term effects are less impressive. What the child appears to learn is that might is right. Delinquents have more commonly been the victims of adult assaults – often of a vicious, persistent and even calculated nature – than the non-delinquents.

Parents who disapprove of aggression and who stop it – but by means other than physical punishment – are least likely to produce aggressive youngsters. Ultimately, an affectionate and tolerant home atmosphere in which adolescents know that aggression is an inappropriate strategy for getting their way, and in which they are able to discriminate the limits beyond which they definitely cannot go, is the best long-term antidote to aggressive behaviour.

Experiments have also demonstrated that a diet of aggressive films increased aggression in adolescent male juvenile delinquents during a specially contrived movie week and in the following period as well. Some of this influence was clearly imitative in nature. The controversy over the effects of television viewing – and, of late, 'video nasties' – on conduct problems such as aggression continues, but the evidence still seems to indicate that exposure to certain categories of television violence occurring in particular settings increases the likelihood of violent actions from already vulnerable (i.e. disturbed) youngsters.

Resolving conflict and preventing problems

One of the factors contributing to the delinquency of many young people is their inability to cope with conflict situations involving authority figures. Conflict situations are those interpersonal situations in which the youth and authority figure (such as a parent or teacher) have opposing desires. The youth may want to buy a motor bike, but his mother wants him to purchase an old car because she thinks bikes are dangerous and will get him bad company. Youngsters often make inappropriate responses to conflict situations (such as fighting, withdrawing, tantrums or destructive behaviour); an escalation of conflict may bring them into contact with clinics, court and other agencies.

Negotiation could sometimes defuse these situations and produce more acceptable consequences for both parties. There are two broad approaches to conflict resolution: (1) arbitration or mediation of specific conflict, and (2) modification of the communication process. Behavioural contracting is the most common form of arbitration; the therapist assumes

'I'd like to see some bloke tell me to go and get my hair cut.'
© Barry Fantoni, reproduced by permission of *The Times*

the role of mediator or arbitrator and thus facilitates mutual agreements between opposing parties about reciprocal exchanges of specific behaviours and reinforcers. These are dealt with in chapter 10. Verbal instructions, practice and feedback are the major techniques used to modify communication process. The emphasis is placed on learning new adaptive behaviours, rather than eliminating problem behaviours, and the techniques are primarily educational rather than therapeutic. These, too, are elaborated in chapter 10.

Prevention within the family, in order to pre-empt the development of antisocial attitudes and behaviour, is the most effective policy available to parents. For instance, we know that moral and social awareness are enhanced by:

1 strong ties of affection and respect between parents and children;
2 firm moral demands made by parents on their offspring;
3 the consistent use of sanctions;
4 techniques of punishment that are psychological rather than physical (e.g. threats to withdraw approval);
5 an intensive use of reasoning and explanations (these are referred to as inductive methods);
6 giving responsibility.

I shall translate these findings into guidelines which you, in turn, can interpret to meet your particular values and the unique circumstances of your family and adolescents.

1 *Foster bonds of respect and affection.* This scarcely needs saying. Such bonds should make all teaching endeavours that much easier; the more affection there is as a foundation for disciplinary tactics, the more notice the youngster will take of what he or she is being told.

2 *Make firm social and moral demands.* Try to establish and convey a reasonably coherent idea of the aims and objectives that lie behind the training and supervision of your teenager. Children whose parents set firm limits for them grow up with more self-esteem and confidence than those who are allowed to get away with behaving in any way they like. It is important to give the youngster a reasonable amount of freedom of choice within those limits.

Teenagers who get their own way all the time interpret such *laissez-faire* permissiveness as indifference. They feel nothing they do is important enough for their parents to bother about. So, if you have to cope with recrimination, invidious comparisons and abuse from your son or daughter, take heart and take the long view. Remain solid and safe; it may be painful for you, but it will pay off in the longer term.

3 *Choose your rules carefully.* Don't make demands for the sake of making demands, rules for the sake of making rules. Any limits set should be for the adolescent's safety, wellbeing, and mature emotional and social development. It is crucial to ensure that teenagers know exactly what the rules and constraints are, and what is expected of them. Rules are most effective when they are relatively uncomplicated, fair, understandable, and applied consistently so that youngsters know what will happen if they break them. No one can advise parents which rules to insist on. Your standards of what is right and wrong, appropriate or inappropriate behaviour, will accord with *your* values and those of your community (or religion) as well as your own philosophy, lifestyle and personality.

4 *Be consistent.* When teaching (or reminding) your teenagers to distinguish between right and wrong, between sensible and unreasonable actions, it is important to be consistent. It is confusing if they are penalized for the way they behave today and get away with the same thing tomorrow. Try not to make idle threats. There's no point in telling your son or daughter, 'You won't go out dancing again if you keep telling lies' when the mother knows she has no choice but to let him or her go to parties and dances.

5 *Be persistent.* Parents often stand out against rebellious, non-compliant behaviour for some time, only to give in eventually. Adolescents, will soon infer that the currency of their parents' words is debased and that if they make a nuisance of themselves for long enough they will be rewarded by getting their own way.

6 *Explain your rules (and discipline) by giving reasons.* Giving explanations is vital to an adolescent's development. It facilitates learning if parents points out the effect of his or her behaviour and give reasons for the restrictions or prohibitions they insist on. Parents, these days, tend to relax their demands for absolute obedience to the rules a little – especially at adolescence – and do not think they are being

demeaned by giving reasons for their expectations. In fact, many parents would regard the giving of explanations as a vital part of the exercise. The rationale might be: 'I wouldn't automatically obey a regulation myself unless I thought there was a good reason for it.' So why not discuss with your teenagers why we must have rules in a complicated social world, what goals they are meant to facilitate, and what would happen if everyone went their own way.

7 *Give your youngster responsibility.* The best way really to learn certain 'lessons' is to be asked to teach them to someone else. This is why the responsibility of (say) looking after a small brother or sister is so valuable in enhancing the social awareness and maturity of the older boy or girl who is doing the substitute parenting.

Chapter Five

Sexual activity

While sexual behaviour has its beginning in infancy and continues throughout childhood, a much broader group of young people engage in sexual activities with greater frequency at the onset of adolescence. New standards have evolved over the last eighty years or so – especially for females – and, in the words of a historian of this subject, 'changes are generally away from a double standard toward a humanized single standard allowing sexual expression in the context of an affectional bond (i.e. when the partners are in love or plan to marry).'

The question has been posed: why, in only sixty or seventy years, has sex in Western life rocketed from unmentionability to almost obsessive public concern? There is no clear answer. But it certainly means that parents who wait until their child's adolescence before beginning sex education have left it in the hands of the media, the school and other children. This is a pity, since learning plays a vital role in sexual practices. Sexual guidance and sex education are important because they help to form the child's and then the adolescent's attitudes towards sex.

The 'stories' we tell ourselves about ourselves matter, for the simple reason that we act on them. This is especially true of our sexual experience and behaviour. Poets, with intricate metaphors, and scientists, with precise and dry technical language, have tried to capture the elusive meanings of terms like 'sex' and 'love'. As cynical adults we may deride such efforts as futile, even self-defeating. But adolescents usually wish to understand the nature of something they feel so powerfully. The difficulty is that sex and love have so many facets, so many hidden qualities and complexities, and mean so many different things to different people, that no wholly satisfactory 'explanations' are ever possible. Nevertheless, our language reflects not only our hidden assumptions, prejudices, myths and stereotypes about sex but also our more explicit ideas, values and attitudes. It actually influences the way we approach, think about and act in sexual relationships.

Sex can be urgent and sensuous, purely erotic, or it can be a spiritual force which is transcendental. At another level, it is merely (or supremely?) a universal biological urge which ensures the continuity of genes, the preservation of a species, its function being to bring about the union of the male sperm and the female ovum. It has a violent and negative side, often being allied with cruelty or sadism. While it can be a joyous and liberating force, it may also be a sad, furtive and shameful act; although it can be an act of love and fulfilment, it can also involve feelings of inferiority, fear and humiliation.

For some adolescents (particularly young boys) sex is thought of as an ephemeral 'thing'; it thus becomes easy to be superficial about it. One can be in love with sex. One can take it or leave it, discard it when it has served its purpose or when it is old and too familiar. Sexual relationships can become an individual selfish matter. The other person's point of view can be conveniently forgotten. Most regrettable of all (some would maintain) is the fact that sex can be compartmentalized, separated from all the other needs, aspirations, attitudes and feelings with which it is usually inextricably interwoven in the psychological make-up of the mature individual. If sex is a thing rather than a loving relationship it can be switched off and on; being sexually aroused then simplifies to finding an attractive sex object.

The nature of male and female sexuality

Sex is usually classified as one of the instincts; it is categorized as such along with hunger and thirst. Because it is seen as a biological need like thirst, this theory about sex makes us think that a denial of sexual gratification should lead to an 'explosive' increase in need. This notion underlies the cold baths and vigorous sports remedies which are suggested to sublimate or purge adolescent sexual energies.

But what does science tell us about sex being an instinct, a biological necessity in the absolute sense? There is no denying that inbuilt or innate physical factors such as hormones and brain mechanisms are important in the sexual behaviour of animals and humans. Of course biological factors do influence sexual behaviour in a number of ways. But scientific evidence also suggests that it is misleading to regard sex in human beings as a simple reaction to biological needs. It is more valid to view sex as an acquired appetite or taste. And this appetite is a product of each individual's experience – his or her unique cultural, social and personal milieu. What we inherit is the capability for sexual arousal and orgasm; the forms and patterns of sex are like other appetites or tastes – they are habits and emotional preferences which have been learned.

The emotional needs and circumstances which promote sexual arousal and satisfactory relationships can vary infinitely. This is not the case with animals. The patterns of courtship and copulation, the stimuli for sexual arousal, are relatively fixed. But as they progress up the evolutionary scale creatures depend less and less on reflex or instinctual patterns of behaviour. It now becomes true to say that sex may be an *emotional* necessity for some people. Promiscuous people are frequently those who have been deprived of love in childhood, and who therefore try to seek emotional security and acceptance through sexual relationships. This is not surprising, since Western society has discovered and exploited the usefulness of sex as an incentive in advertising. For others sex is not an imperative; it is subservient to or co-equal to other needs, motives and behaviours.

Sexual attitudes and needs take many forms, then, and the patterns are fairly well established by the late teens. Of course they will be elaborated and, indeed, modified with greater maturity. The 'problems' related to sex, in the secondary school, are likely to be due to sexual curiosity and ignorance. Even in our supposedly enlightened age, one is impressed by the anguish and disappointment caused by widespread misinformation, misconceptions, myths, fears and inhibitions about sex. 'If only I had been given more information about these things when I was young' is still a sentiment to be heard by parents today, quite often from young adults.

The problem for parents, apart from shyness about sex shared by so many in our culture, may be that they simply misunderstand the way in which the word 'sex' is used by most sex educators. Sex has a far wider meaning and function than is popularly attributed to it. Those who deny that the infant has any sex life commonly do so because they imagine, when it is suggested that the very small child is affected by sex, that this must necessarily be a comparable experience to that of the adult. This denial leads to sex education being put off until adolescence, and then (perhaps out of embarrassment) shelved entirely.

By the time puberty arrives, triggered by an interaction between the sex hormones and certain cells of the brain, psychosexual development and differentiation between males and females in their identity with their gender are well developed and largely irreversible. In fact, by the age of 7, a child is passionately committed to shaping his or her behaviour to the cultural mould of what is thought 'appropriate' to his or her biological sex. Once the standards of sex-role behaviour are learned, they are not easily altered.

Immense changes occur at puberty, and the maturing of the sex glands is of great consequence at this stage. Even more important, however, is the convergence of critical emotional and social developments which have been taking place since childhood, and which reach maturity now. Tensions and indefinable longings are aroused by the awakening sex drive.

We saw in chapter 1 that puberty is the point in life at which sexual maturity begins, marked in girls by the first menstrual flow and in boys by a number of signs, the most reliable probably being the presence of spermatozoa in the urine (detectable under the microscope). When puberty begins, the parent soon knows all about it; and it may be at any time after the age of 11 that the trouble starts. In the case of a boy, almost overnight the erstwhile 'child' becomes moody and preoccupied, and parents find it more and more difficult to predict how he will behave. One day he's chatty and friendly and the next day withdrawn and secretive; now he's grateful for parents' help, then fiercely resentful of their interference. The boy is caught up in forces he doesn't understand – the turbulence of biological change. At one instant he is elated, and then suddenly depressed; confident in his powers, then overwhelmed by feelings of inadequacy.

It is not being suggested that girls are immune from such experiences. But there are some differences between the sexes in the way sexuality affects them. There is little question that for a majority of boys the rapid increase in sexual drive that accompanies adolescence is imperious and biologically specific and therefore difficult, if not impossible, to deny. Sexual activity in general, and masturbation in particular, are considerably greater among boys than girls. Among girls, for reasons that are poorly understood, the sexual drive is likely to be somewhat more diffuse and ambiguous at first. Their sexuality may, for a limited period, be capable of being denied, or transformed and displaced into other channels and other guises. It may be idealized, romanticized, even stripped (for a while) of its physical and erotic connotations. The same sort of thing does occur with boys, but it tends to happen less often.

There is nothing absolute about these distinctions; they represent statistical generalizations or average differences. The girls' attitudes to activities are doubtless influenced by society's more restrictive prohibitions and judgements about the sexual mores appropriate to females as compared with males. This is still reflected in wide differences from culture to culture in what young men and women think and do about their sexuality.

Early sexual activity: masturbation and homosexual play

Most industrialized and monotheistic cultures train children not to masturbate. It seems to be a training which almost universally breaks down at adolescence and even before then, particularly in the case of boys. There is considerable emotional reaction to masturbation from mothers. Although most modern mothers have heard, read or personally experienced the fact that masturbation is harmless and that it does not stunt growth, or cause insanity, sterility or impotence, they may feel anxious when their children do it.

Like most behaviours, masturbation, if carried to an extreme, can become a problem, or may be symptomatic of an already existing problem. Many children who are deprived, unhappy and poorly adjusted turn to masturbation as a source of comfort and relief from tension. It is the compulsive element which is a sign that all is not well with the child's emotional and social development. And here professional guidance is advisable.

In pre-adolescent individuals, sexual interest and behaviour are intermittent, casual and not very intense. Sexual experimentation, mainly sex play between children of the same sex, rises in incidence as youngsters get older. Homosexual play usually takes the form of handling each other's genitals. This occurs in roughly 30 per cent of 13-year-olds. We know from surveys that about one in two adults is likely to have had one or more sexually tinged experiences involving someone of the same sex, and that at least half of those who haven't have felt some sexual attraction to someone of their own sex. Usually the attraction or contact is a one-off matter which mainly occurs during adolescence. Homosexual activities are much more common in boys' and girls' boarding schools than in day schools, but there is no convincing evidence that this transient phase of homosexual activity has any bearing on *long-term* adult homosexuality. However, personal circumstances and the presence or absence of opportunities for heterosexual contacts influence the manifestation of homosexual activities.

What can we infer from all this sexual experimentation in the early adolescent phase of development? It seems clear that we cannot suppress children's sexual interests and explorations, even if we should want to do so. It has been argued that the only effect of extreme efforts at suppression is to drive the behaviour underground and to permeate it with a sense of shame and an aura of furtive excitement. In girls, the harsh suppression of sexuality during childhood and adolescence is one of the main contributory causes of sexual inhibition in adulthood.

First relationships with the opposite sex

Early approaches to the opposite sex may be clumsy and (in the case of boys) somewhat aggressive and uncouth. A boy's mother may be subjected to aggression, as her son tries to express his growing independence as well as the feelings of frustration, inadequacy and strangeness he so intensely experiences. Later, in many boys, feelings towards both girlfriend and mother tend to become more tender, chivalrous and sometimes tinged with idealism. Girls may enjoy being flirtatious with their fathers, enjoying their ability to 'get around' them in a way that their mothers sometimes find irritatingly manipulative. To the mother's chagrin, she may sense a little jealousy and rivalry towards the vital young woman emerging from childhood. It is important that adolescents, already feeling vulnerable, are not ridiculed when they show all the feverish signs of calf love. They have enough lessons to learn about the opposite sex, about their role in an adult world, and so on, without the added burden of unsympathetic resentment or teasing.

The attainment of sexual maturity has a profound effect upon adolescents' status among those of their own age. Early-maturing boys and girls look grown up for their age and are thus given more responsibility by adults. They are likely to become leaders and to participate widely in school clubs and activities. They find it easier to compete and win at sport. Their self-confidence is boosted, and so is their popularity. Yet sometimes the strain of being different, of being expected to behave, begins to tell.

Boys tend to cope with early maturing more easily than girls; their early maturity puts them on a par with girls of the same age. Girls, in particular, may find that their early maturity is sexually provocative to others. They may be self-conscious about their precocious sexual development, especially their body image and the fact of menstruation. Premature sexual development seldom means premature sexual outlets of an adult kind. In general, premature puberty leads to an increase in sexual arousal, but psychosexual behaviour tends to remain roughly in line with the child's actual age and social experience.

Late maturers look childlike for their age. They are more likely to be teased by their peers and thus beset by feelings of inferiority and a sense of social isolation. Girls are likely to suffer less than boys because they are on a par with most boys of their own age, but they may worry about late breast development and the start of their periods, particularly if under pressure from their more physically advanced peers. Boys who are late developers seem to feel the most pressure and lack most in self-confidence.

British boys and girls begin to 'go out' with the opposite sex somewhat later than their American counterparts, where 'dating' as a social institution (backed at times by parental pressure) creates powerful expectations of not always enthusiastic young teenagers. The net result is that by the age of 13 a significant proportion of American adolescents will have had their first date. While young girls, at first, show interest in boys of their own age, they turn in their early teens to what seem more interesting and mature older boys for attention, and older boys, in turn, interest themselves in younger girls.

It may surprise parents to learn that surveys reveal a tendency for boys and girls to look for qualities in a partner that are remarkably in keeping with what is their own view of desirable traits in a potential partner. They include mental and physical fitness, dependability, good manners and personal appearance, clean speech and actions, a pleasant disposition, a sense of humour, consideration and 'acting one's age'.

Parents of young adolescents sometimes become concerned if a relationship becomes too serious, in the sense of having the status of courtship (i.e. a commitment to marriage). They tend to feel their teenagers are too young 'to know their own mind' and should have the chance to meet others, not to mention having more time to enjoy their short-lived youth and to develop more maturity.

The problem of defining a lasting love relationship is of great importance to parents whose youngster is courting seriously. Romantic love, as the basis of marriage, is a relatively modern concept and is widely accepted only in Western countries. Harmonizing the modern concept of romantic love with the lifelong partnership that is marriage has proved to be one of the major challenges to contemporary Western society. Some people feel that marriage and the family are burdens too heavy (and too serious) for an 'ephemeral' relationship such as romantic love to sustain. Others believe that individual choice made on the basis of romantic feelings can lead to lasting relationships. The psychiatrist Dr J. Dominion, an expert on marriage and marital problems, states that the survival of every marriage depends on the capacity of the partners to meet the psychological needs of the other, which in turn requires a fair degree of maturity. He suggests that a mature relationship is based on mutual understanding and equality between the partners. Authority, power and decision-making are shared. This emphasis on equality and maturity explains many parents' anxiety when their offspring make what they see as a too early commitment to marriage. Their intuitive fears are correct. The marriages of very young people tend not to be successful. The high rate of divorce in young marriages is even higher than the rate of divorces in general. So many marriages will falter or fail that nearly one-quarter of the babies born in the UK today are likely to experience a separation of their parents before they reach school-leaving age.

Sexual intercourse in adolescence

Having boyfriends or girlfriends can be the source of feelings of insecurity, not only for a lot of young people, but also for parents, who may worry about some of the implications of their offspring's newly awakened sexual feelings. Parents in general express more conservative, traditional attitudes than their adolescent sons or daughters on such topics as petting and, notably, premarital sexual intercourse, whether the couple intend to marry or not. The size of the minority of adults who approve of sexual intercourse between engaged couples is considerably smaller than the percentage of these same adults who themselves had premarital sexual relations. It would be uncharitable to call this 'hypocrisy' rather than 'selective amnesia'. Of course, parents are not necessarily being hypocritical or puritanical if they disapprove of (or have reservations about) teenagers having sex. Many are afraid that young people might be hurt or exploited if they embark on a sexual relationship too soon. It can be difficult to sustain a sexual relationship if the adolescent – who, by definition, is short on experience – has not yet learned to maintain intimacy in a non-sexual attachment.

Unfortunately, there is a lack of really satisfactory comparative data which might be used to assess changes in sexual attitudes and behaviour over time. Nevertheless (as Professor Michael Rutter's 1979 review of studies indicates) there is little doubt that in the UK and the USA adolescents engage in sexual activity at a younger age than their predecessors.

Whatever today's mothers and fathers may say to the social scientists when they come to the door armed with their surveys, one gets the distinct impression that parents are generally philosophical about (or resigned to) this relatively precocious sexuality. While there is an apparently inexorable tendency for most parents to become more conservative with age, we *are* referring here to a generation that was young in the 1960s, a decade associated with the liberalization of sexual attitudes and easier access to effective contraception.

Has the relatively recent media obsession or the discovery

of the pill for birth control led to radical new attitudes towards sexuality among adolescents? There is a widespread view that since the 1960s there have been dramatic changes amounting to a revolution in the sexual attitudes and actions of young people. We have seen that teenagers enjoy the full range of sexual activities earlier than the previous generation. The number of teenage pregnancies has certainly increased markedly, despite innovations in contraception. The incidence of venereal disease among young people has also gone up.

Although adolescents have become more accepting in their attitudes to premarital sex, this does not imply a massive rise in casual sexual relationships. Young people, and particularly girls, continue to emphasize the importance of love and stable emotional attachment in premarital sex, although intended marriage or an engagement is not so often seen as a prerequisite of such relationships. The emphasis on a stable relationship with one sexual partner at a time is referred to as 'serial monogamy'. Girls do, however, display more conservative attitudes to these issues than boys.

Most youngsters wish to get married and have children. Certainly, a committed relationship is generally thought to be essential for the rearing of children, and, although a majority would wish such a longstanding commitment to take the form of marriage, a substantial minority reject such a view. An American study, by psychologist Dr R. C. Sorensen in 1973, indicated that a majority of teenagers expect sexual fidelity after marriage, even though they do not expect it before then. There is no evidence that this view has changed.

Surveys suggest that the first experience of sexual intercourse is usually with someone who is already experienced; the first partner is often older and, in the case of the girls, is quite often an adult. Intercourse is usually with a friend and, more often than not, takes place in the parental home of the beginner or the partner. The first experience (according to Dr M. Schofield's interviews with English adolescents in the 1960s) was often unpremeditated and unplanned, and a majority said they did not enjoy it. Shame and fear were common reactions experienced by girls, disappointment the predominant reaction of boys. (Nevertheless, within a month, 54 per cent of the boys and 61 per cent of the girls had tried again.) Boys described their first experience of sexual intercourse as being impelled by sexual desire, while most girls gave love as the reason. Unfortunately we do not have more recent findings based upon really large-scale surveys of this kind.

Premarital sexual relations are a long way from being universal among teenagers. On the other hand, it is equally apparent that adolescent premarital intercourse is not something to be dismissed as a minority activity confined to a few 'deviates'; it is common enough to be seen as one manifestation of adolescent conformity. Despite the physical and social pressures (teenagers desire to be like other teenagers) towards sexual intercourse, many adolescents manage to resist these influences.

A historical perspective reveals that a recent sexual revolution is something of a myth. The real changes in the ages at which adolescents initiate sexual activity have been gradual and taking place since the early part of this century. There has always been a sex difference in adolescent values, with boys more likely to seek sexual 'adventures' with a variety of partners and girls more likely to seek a 'romantic' relationship with one partner. There has been a long-term trend, occurring over several decades, towards placing a high value on premarital sexual intercourse with one partner. Young people – like most adults – expect fidelity from their partners. Forty per cent of the sample in Schofield's (1973) study of young adults in the UK either had no sexual experience prior to marriage or had had experience with only the person he or she ultimately married.

Clinical evidence suggests that teenagers are as secretive and wary about sex as ever. Most adolescents (according to surveys) believe that they have sexual problems of one kind or another, and many comment on the intense anxiety they suffer. Harmonious sexual relationships are relatively infrequent. Even today there are teenagers who worry about masturbation, and nearly all boys and two-thirds of girls will masturbate by the age of 16. The strength of these wishes and impulses is often alarming to the young adolescent. The desire to display the strength or beauty of one's body, to have it admired and desired, usually produces feelings of guilt, feelings which, as we have seen before, originate in the fantasies and activities of earlier periods of life, and in the traditional attitudes of parents, schools, and so on.

Such feelings of guilt are frequently aroused by the awareness of having become a real competitor with the parents of one's own sex. The adolescent boy or girl's awareness of being the equal or superior of the father or mother in terms of physical strength or beauty, sexual attraction or intellectual ability can create enormous conflicts in the adolescent. Excessive shyness may serve the purpose of denying the existence of such possibilities and of preventing their ever assuming reality. With such behaviour, adolescents virtually assure their parents of their harmlessness. Again, a long period of time may be needed to work through to the guiltless conviction of being entitled to be admired, to have intimate relations with the opposite sex and to explore everything that (until then) has been a prerogative of the adult world.

Michael Rutter reminds us that sexual competence and experience can be hard won. As he puts it:

> Sexual behaviour includes many learned components and depending upon whether a person's first sexual experience is enjoyable or unpleasant he may not try again for many years or he may have intercourse again within a few days and continue to have sex regularly and frequently. . . . Sexual intercourse tends to be most pleasurable within the context of a long relationship, emphasizing that sexuality and socialization are linked.

Sex education

It is quite likely that parents are the last people teenagers can discuss their sexual problems with, because of parental inhibitions, the teenager's inhibitions or a mixture of both. Does it matter if parents are unable to talk to their teenagers about this sometimes fraught subject? Those parents who are able to establish good lines of communication with their children would certainly answer in the affirmative. If it is important to discuss education, employment, morality, politics and a thousand and one other things with one's children, why ever not sex? And there are many important issues – such as the possibilities of pregnancy, disease, premature commitment to an unsuitable partner – to which inexperienced young people should be alerted.

What children do about sexual relationships as they approach sexual maturity will depend on their education about sex during the years of childhood. And this means education not only about the 'facts of life' but about sexual morality, the obligations human beings have to one another, and ideals and values such as respect, responsibility and love.

But do you find it easy to discuss contraception with your son or daughter, or does it raise the spectre (unacceptable, perhaps, to you) of an admission that they *are* actually having sex? Are you concerned that your youngster is wrestling with problems over his feelings about the opposite sex – that he shows homosexual inclinations? If so, how on earth do you broach such a delicate matter? The most difficult topics in sex education are those which involve the kind of exploitation and violence that occur in pornography, prostitution, rape and incest. These subjects have been included in the references in the 'Further reading' section.

The type of questions that teenagers ask – 'Is it all right for me to have sex?', 'Should I be using contraception?', 'What is a perversion?', 'Is it wrong to masturbate?', 'What are venereal diseases?', 'What is a homosexual?', 'How do you get AIDS?', 'Should I go to a family planning clinic?', 'What is an orgasm?', 'What is a wet dream?', 'Does it hurt when the hymen is broken?', 'What is abnormal sex?', 'How do you say no?' – highlights one of the fundamental difficulties of sex education, particularly in schools, where the audience is composed of adolescents from different home backgrounds, whose religious, ethical and moral training may differ quite considerably. Some questions can be answered 'scientifically', as matters of biological information. Others involve moral and personal values. Should a teacher (or for that matter a parent) go further and explain not only the biological elements of sex but also the whole complex of love life? After all, many would believe that sexuality, in the full sense, is part of a consistent philosophy of life, part of a whole lifestyle, not something encapsulated and separate.

Although sex education should preferably be initiated before adolescence (as I stated at the beginning of the chapter), assistance and support should still be given. Several specialist publications on the subject are listed in the reference section of a good local library and, in this book, under the heading 'Further reading'.

Here I offer some guidelines for your own efforts at sex education:

1 Provide an understanding of the biological and anatomical facts that form the basis of sexual activity.
2 Explain how other psychological, emotional, social and moral elements play a part in responsible sexual relationships.
3 Try to eliminate fears and misconceptions about the changes of puberty and sexual activity (there are still youngsters who believe that heavy petting can lead to pregnancy).
4 Encourage a positive and healthy (as opposed to ashamed and furtive) attitude to sexual matters.
5 Explain about the dangers of venereal and other diseases.
6 Explain about the risk of pregnancy.
7 Take active steps to provide practical advice or action with regard to contraception. Granted that this is an emotive issue and a highly personal choice, nevertheless it *is* the major issue in adolescent sexual activity. The possibility of pregnancy has to be faced.
8 Explain the nature of homosexuality.

Films, special talks and lectures can be very helpful in the sex education process. But only you, knowing your child, are able to answer the supplementary questions that are almost always asked (sometimes much later and only after information has been digested). Only you can fit the biological facts into the chosen system of values. The following information on guidelines 5–8 should assist you in your efforts to impart knowledge to your teenager.

Sexually transmitted and related diseases

The adage 'prevention is better than cure' is certainly not platitudinous when alerting sexually active adolescents to the importance of genital hygiene and the risks of sexually transmitted diseases (see 'Further reading'). These are on the increase. Individuals court above-average risks if they have more than one sexual partner, or if their partner makes love to one or more other persons. And the risk is high for promiscuous youngsters – that is, if they have several partners, each of whom, in turn, makes love to several people.

Genital hygiene is a significant preventive health-care strategy; being scrupulous about sexual partners is another. The major sexually transmitted diseases are gonorrhoea ('dose', 'clap', or 'drip'), syphilis, and genital herpes. AIDS (Acquired Immune Deficiency Syndrome) can be transmitted sexually,. but is also contracted through blood by such people as haemophiliacs and drug users. Other related diseases are scabies and pubic lice. These are contracted through close physical contact, and can therefore be contracted by *sleeping* with someone with the disease, but not through sexual intercourse itself.

There is not space here to describe the symptoms of each of these conditions. It is wise for the youngster to visit the doctor if he or she complains of pain or burning sensations when passing urine, unusual discharges from penis or vagina, sores, bumps or rashes or small organisms in the genital area, fevers and other signs of being unwell.

Contraception

Whether we like it or not, the inescapable implication of adolescent sexual activity is the risk of an unwanted pregnancy. This, in turn, raises psychological and moral dilemmas for the boy and girl and their parents. Untold harm may be caused if the pregnant teenager feels impelled by social or parental pressure, but against her personal inclinations, to undergo an abortion or to have the baby, or if the couple are forced into an unsuitable marriage. Such early marriages tend to do badly, and an unwanted child could get off to a very unpromising start in life.

Of course Catholic and, indeed, many non-Catholic parents may have religious and moral scruples about contraception and all that it implies. But, in the light of the facts – that a large proportion of young people do enjoy regular sexual intercourse – is it not ostrich-like to refuse to consider the possibility of unwanted pregnancies and to advise teenagers about the responsible precautions they might adopt?

The following information should assist you if you decide to discuss this matter with your teenager. Table 1 (from an excellent guide by writer/researcher Kay Wellings) indicates the relative effectiveness of various contraceptive methods, expressed in terms of the number of women out of a hundred who would get pregnant using the method for a whole year. The perfect method (apart from total abstinence) would have a failure rate of 0 out of 100.

Interestingly, a 1980s survey of young people's attitudes towards contraception, carried out by the British Health Education Council, showed that 78 per cent saw contraception as a joint affair, and 82 per cent maintained that a man should always ask a woman about contraception before assuming it was safe to have sex. Sadly, much of this thoughtfulness proves to be mere lip-service when translated into practice.

The pill, which is most popular with younger women today, contains synthetic hormones – a progestogen, which makes the womb an environment that is hostile to sperm, and also, in the case of the combined pill, an oestrogen, which prevents the release of eggs, that is to say inhibits ovulation. It is essential that the pills are taken correctly according to instructions.

Table 1 *Playing safe: a league table*

Method	Failure rate (pregnancies per 100 women using method regularly for 1 year)	Effectiveness
Combined pill	0.3/100	Over 99% when correctly used
Mini-pill	2/100	98% when correctly used
Sheath	3/100	85–98%
Cap/diaphragm	3/100	85–97%
IUD	2–4/100	96–9%
Sponge	15–20/100	75–91%
Withdrawal or spermicides only	17–25/100	75–83%
Nothing	90/100	–

Source: Family Planning Association and Kay Wellings (1986), *First Sex, First Love* (Wellingborough: Thorsons)

Is the pill safe? Some four out of ten women report side-effects, including nausea, headaches, weight gain and, in some cases, mood changes such as depression. Some of these problems may clear up after a few months of regular use. Many women find an advantage in taking the pill because of its tendency to relieve menstrual problems such as pain, irregularity and heaviness. The pill is related to some serious side-effects, including an *increased risk* of high blood pressure and blood clotting (particularly in older women); some studies have also linked it with cervical or breast cancer. Other studies argue that the pill actually protects users against cancer of the womb, arthritis and other conditions. The health issues are not simple and are best discussed frankly with your daughter and family doctor. Today, more lower-dose and progestogen-only pills are prescribed than in the past; it may put things in perspective if we remind ourselves that these long-term risks are much less than those so readily embraced when people (and a worryingly high proportion of young people) choose to smoke.

Barrier methods physically prevent the male sperm from reaching the woman's cervix or womb. They include the *sheath* ('french letter' or condom), which is the only contraceptive method available to men which doesn't prevent them from eventually becoming fathers (as is the case with vasectomy, a sterilization procedure).

The *cap* and *diaphragm* – similar but separate barrier methods – fit over the cervix so that sperm cannot reach the egg in the womb and fertilize it. The device is inserted by the user herself and should always be used in conjunction with a spermicide. The initial fitting, however, and advice about use, must be obtained from a family planning clinic or family doctor. These methods carry virtually no harmful side-effects; however, they are messy and distasteful to some women.

The sponge is a newcomer to the range of barrier methods. It is a marshmallow-like substance which is attached to a ribbon; it fits over the cervix, having been soaked with spermicide. This method is more flexible, figuratively speaking, in its application than the cap and diaphragm (the sponge can be left in place for up to 30 hours); but it has a higher failure rate.

The intra-uterine device (IUD), popularly known as the coil or loop, has definite drawbacks for young, single people; doctors do not consider them suitable because of the increased risk of infection leading to infertility.

Spermicides – creams, jellies, foams and pessaries – are contraceptives with a high failure rate if used alone.

Coping with an unplanned pregnancy

The first sign of pregnancy is, of course, a missed period. The surest way of finding out is a pregnancy test carried out by the doctor or a pregnancy advice service.

It is to be hoped that a pregnant teenager will have the kind of relationship with her parents which allows her to confide in them. What happens then, the decisions made and actions taken, can be painful. Kay Wellings makes the point that

> as with many other controversial issues, we may hold very strong views on the subject until we're personally involved, and then we may start to feel very differently. A woman who has previously been a firm defender of the rights of the unborn child may find herself wavering when her own life is in danger of disruption. Contrawise, the stalwart supporter of abortion on demand may feel differently when a baby is growing inside her own body.

Wise counselling is imperative in such a complex and often fraught situation. There are several organizations offering counselling services and providing practical help (see 'Further reading' for books offering specialist advice and addresses).

A decision to go ahead with the pregnancy will depend on the answers to questions, some involving moral values, others to do with plain, practical and factual matters.

1 What are the moral attitudes towards, and feelings for, the unborn child (embryo or foetus)?
2 What is the moral or emotional attitude towards abortion?
3 What were the couple intending to do with their lives?
4 How stable is their relationship?
5 Did they have a commitment to live together and (at some time) begin a family?
6 What is their (her) financial position; access to housing, if
   (a) they wish to raise the child as a couple, in their home?
   (b) she wishes to raise the child as a single parent either in her own home or in her parents' home?
7 What is the level of emotional maturity and physical resources they (she) will bring to a parental role?
8 Are the couple (and their families) prepared to arrange for the baby to be fostered or adopted?

There are two vital questions. What is in the baby-to-be's best interests? What is in the parents' best interests? These are not always easy to reconcile.

Homosexual relationships

Deep-seated homosexuality/lesbianism (distinguished from the superficial, transient homosexual activities of early adolescence), which is a sexual preference for persons of the same sex, is quite likely to be recognized (and put into words as such) by the individual during adolescence. For some a dawning awareness of being 'different' may come before the teens. The consciousness of being truly homosexual comes to some in early adolescence, for others only in the later teens. Counsellors urge caution when young people express concern about their sexual orientation at 13 or 14 years of age because of the commonness of transient homosexual activity. Crushes on the same sex (as I indicated earlier) are a fairly normal feature of pre- and early adolescent development. The less ephemeral form of homosexuality is quite likely to be denied at first, pushed back into unconsciousness.

Homosexuality appears to be a universal phenomenon, tolerated to a greater or lesser degree by societies at different periods of history or in different parts of the world. Some societies have used taboos, social conventions and legislation to prevent homosexual relationships.

A great deal of personal suffering is caused when parents or others react punitively towards the homosexual who has 'come out' and acknowledged the inevitable. Trying to hide homosexuality causes intolerable stress and unhappiness. Criticism and rejection have always proved ineffective, for there is little evidence that a person can change what he or she is, and certainly what they cannot help. There is no evidence that society can ever legislate human variations in love out of existence.

Being homosexual ('gay') or heterosexual ('straight') does not always indicate an either/or sexual status. Homosexuality and heterosexuality represent opposite ends of a spectrum (or continuum) of sexual behaviours along which individuals might find themselves. Some people do not feel able to label themselves as clearly heterosexual or homosexual; they may enjoy sexual relationships with both men and women. There is commonly some confusion about the traits attributed to homosexual men and women, the former being perceived as 'effeminate', the latter as 'butch' or 'masculine'. In fact, homosexual males may be 'macho' or effeminate, or anything in between these extreme and imprecise stereotypes; lesbians, likewise, may manifest every variation between 'mannish' and 'womanly' qualities, just as do heterosexual people.

One often hears it said that homosexuality is on the increase in our society. It may be more visible because of our more tolerant attitudes and laws, but there is no evidence that the incidence of homosexuality alters significantly from generation to generation. In our society it is estimated that one in ten people is fairly exclusively homosexual, with a smaller proportion of women than men showing gay preferences.

It is now generally recognized (although many people have misgivings or prejudices about the subject) that people who prefer same-sex sex are not ill, physically or mentally. Their relationships with their lovers and partners (many being partnerships for life) span just as wide a spectrum as do straight relationships.

It is easy to advise parents, but difficult for them to accept (particularly if they have religious and other personal scruples concerning homosexuality) that, if they wish to maintain their child's bond of love and respect, they have little choice but to be philosophical, sympathetic and supportive. Where change may be possible with professional help, *if* change is really desired, it is in the case of the bisexual individual who enjoys emotional and sexual relationships with the opposite sex as well as his or her own. What is clear is that homosexual adolescents of either sex do not choose to be gay. They may choose *not* to be by suppressing or hiding their sexual orientation, some to the point of entering into a heterosexual marriage. The results of concealment and desperate remedies are usually a disaster. It is not easy, but doubtless it is best to accept what one is.

Chapter Six

Leaving school: work and unemployment

The mere fact of having a job is significant for individuals' development in late adolescence. The practical experience of working is thought to bring adolescence to an end. The choice of the right occupation is also of vital importance, not least because most people spend about one-third of their lives at work. That chosen (or 'unchosen') occupation – we do not always have a real choice – and its socio-economic status in adult life will be significantly influenced by the adolescent's formal education and academic success.

Choosing an occupation

Children and adolescents frequently face questions about their future work role such as 'What are you going to be when you grow up?' or 'What will you do when you leave school?' The very form of the question implies that occupation determines a person's identity. In fact, the work role is probably the most important factor in the development of his or her self-identity, and the factor most directly involved in the young person's crisis of identity, if there is one. The choice of work is one of the most difficult commitments a young person must make. According to Erik Erikson (1968), the inability to settle on an occupational identity can be one of the most disturbing problems for young people.

According to some theorists, the central process in career choice is the development and implementation of an individual's vocational self-concept. Vocational self-concepts are more or less integrated with youngsters' other developing concepts of themselves. They have to explore choices actively by means of information about the favoured occupation, but also by means of occupational role-playing (imagining themselves as teacher, social worker, doctor or nurse) in the evolution of this self-image. It must be purposeful, realistic and in keeping with their abilities, if it is to be effective.

The majority of teenagers make their initial choice of occupation when they are at school. The information and guidance provided by teachers and others play an important part in the making of decisions. The term 'decision-making' is rather grand when one considers what actually happens to many young people. It implies careful 'research' and thoughtful deliberation. Despite all that is at stake, people often choose their jobs because of some fortuitous influence rather than as a result of a painstaking review of the occupational field.

Studies carried out in various parts of Britain on the ways in which pupils choose their occupations have produced consistent results. While intensely held occupational ambitions are unusual, the majority of youngsters have established fairly firm preferences by their final year at school. Such stability of preference does not generally result from any systematic consideration of alternatives. Choices, particularly among working-class children, are determined often by chance factors such as the occupations of uncles and aunts, or the casual remarks of friends about their jobs.

An American psychologist, O. E. Thompson, in a 1971 study of the occupational values of high school students as freshmen and later as sophomores, was able to show that the characteristics of a vocation that was important to them may have been internalized relatively early in life. They may, indeed, have been well established upon entering high school; such characteristics may not change readily.

A popular theory suggests that occupational choice falls into three psychological phases:

1 The *fantasy* period coincides with the child's primary (or elementary) school experiences and involves fantasy

choices (doctor, space pilot, nurse, jet pilot) which are emotional rather than practical. They exist in the child's world of play and daydreaming.

2 The *tentative* period, from the ages of 11–17, is when the boy or girl gradually shifts towards reality and his or her interests play a major role. The youngster begins to consider his or her education, aptitudes, personal values and goals and tries to match them to the interests.

3 The *realistic* period finds the adolescent assessing his or her aspirations, motivations and the requirements of the job wanted. The teenager's objective is then pursued by vocational and educational planning.

Phase 3 makes the choice sound like a very rational and conscious process. In fact, it is somewhat more haphazard.

Peter March (an adviser on careers and education) and Michael Smith (a headmaster), authors of a series of *Your Choice* books, put forward the various choices British children face in their school careers:

at 14+, deciding to continue some subjects and drop others;
at 16+, deciding to remain at school, work or opt for further education;
at 18+, deciding to stay at school for a third-year sixth; to move to higher education; to go to work; to start on a sandwich course; or to take a year off.

The late 1970s (when the British Careers Research and Advisory Centre published this book) were more optimistic times. One of the 'options' today is to leave school and find oneself, despite one's best efforts, unemployed. This is a probability rather than a mere threat to many youngsters with limited qualifications, few social connections, or a home in an area of high unemployment. They feel there is no chance for them long before they have had the opportunity to try the shrunken labour market.

In January 1981 nearly 20 per cent (1 in 5) of under 18-year-olds in the British labour market were jobless, compared with 7.4 per cent of school-leavers in October 1979. In 1981–2 one in two teenagers leaving school at 16 went into the Youth Opportunities Programme because they could not find employment. This scheme was replaced by the Youth Training Scheme and a number of other ventures to provide youngsters with basic training.

In Europe and the USA there are particular areas of high unemployment where youths face the same dilemmas as in the UK. Many skilled and semiskilled jobs once held by adolescents have been eliminated by automation or the drastic reduction in manufacturing industries. The number of *meaningful* work experiences for teenagers is meagre. Many of the jobs that are available are drearily routine and of little usefulness to the young worker.

Teachers have told me how adversely such pessimism affects the morale, motivation and discipline within the classroom. How do you appeal to a boy or girl to work harder in order to get a good job, when they know that however much they strive it is likely to be the 'dole queue' for them, which implies to many of them that they are being consigned to the scrap heap before they could get started and prove themselves? The blight of being excluded from normal working experiences without even the expectation of knowing their joys and sorrows, advantages and disadvantages, has destructive consequences. The chapter dealing with disruptive, underachieving students describes the demoralization, resentment and (for some) apathy which is symptomatic of a sense of hopelessness about the future. Youth Training Schemes may offer a palliative but scarcely make up for 'a proper job with prospects'.

In talking about 'occupational choice' there is an assumption that the job one acquires is determined by some combination of the preferences, desires, abilities and aspirations of the person for a particular occupational status. But there are additional factors (other than unemployment) over which the individual has little or no control, the most obvious and significant of these being race. It is a depressing fact that, other things being equal (aptitude, suitability for the job), the white boy or girl in Britain may have a better chance of being appointed than the black or Asian applicant. Women, too, can be disadvantaged when competing with men for many jobs; while the disabled often face considerable difficulties.

For the more fortunate adolescent students (as they prepare to leave school) there are (according to March and Smith), mixed feelings:

1 Some will wish to sort out their lifestyle first.
2 Some will want to keep their options open.
3 Some will want to earn money right away.
4 Some will know exactly what they want to do.
5 Some will be completely undecided.
6 Some will be restless.

These career advisers describe several possible courses of action (see table 2), matching options against prevailing states of mind.

Let us consider those youngsters who remain undecided about what to do. What can be done (or should have been done) to help them formulate their plans for their future careers?

It is usually thought that preparing youngsters for their adult vocations is a major preoccupation with schools, so one might expect their educational experiences to affect the occupations they choose – and to some extent they do. Much of the research into occupational preference and choice has been based on the idea that the occupations which people choose and enjoy vary according to their personal characteristics, for example their interests and abilities. There is, after all, a substantial relationship between having an interest in a job and the quality of one's performance. Such interests tend to be relatively changeable until the late teens. Aptitude for particular kinds of work is, of course, very important too.

Studies of how childrearing, parental and personality factors influence occupational choice tend to be ambiguous and unhelpful. A large-scale (1968) survey by psychologist Charles Werts of over 76,000 young American men did, however, reveal a strong tendency for students (in college) to enter their fathers' occupations or occupations closely related to those of their fathers.

Table 2 *Starting points for the 18+ decision*

Possible courses of action	*Decided*	*Undecided*	*Keep options open*	*Restless*	*Money now*
Third-year sixth	The third-year sixth does not automatically solve all your problems.	The third-year sixth is not a device to put off making decisions.	An effective measure providing the results at the end will be better than after year two.	Not a good move if you have had enough of your present environment.	This move is a loser if cash is crucial!
Higher education	Have you fully checked out on course comparisons before applying?	To see the wood for the trees, ask yourself whether you would prefer theoretical or vocational training.	Have you considered the new Diploma in Higher Education? Ideal for keeping doors open.	You will be well advised to sort out your problems first before committing yourself to a college.	It is still a viable possibility to work your way through college, polytechnic or university.

Employment	Are you cutting yourself off from training which may affect your future promotion?	Look before you leap if you are not sure. A false move now could prejudice future applications.	The larger and more diverse the firm, the wider will be the employment opportunities.	An employer might not be as tolerant of the restless as the school or student world.	The obvious winner – but try to pick an employer who will offer training on and off the job.
Sandwich course	Have you investigated all sources of industrial bursaries?	How do you see yourself 10 years hence? That answer may help your decision now.	The broader the framework of the course, the more flexible the training.	Getting involved with theory as well as practice could be a useful solution.	Find out all you can about the financial benefits from industrially sponsored ventures.
Year off	Have you balanced all the pros and cons of taking a year off?	Obtain some consumer reaction from someone who has experienced it.	A good possibility providing you plan the next step during the year rather than at the end of it.	This is a possible way of working out dis-ease but make sure it does not prolong it.	The majority of students do not make a fortune but many make enough to get by for the year.

Source: P. March and M. Smith (1977), *Your Choice at 17+* (Cambridge: Hobsons Press)

It is well established that the advice and information provided by parents is more influential than that provided from other sources. Can you help your son or daughter make a rational choice of career and occupation? The trouble is that, even if young people try to survey the whole range of occupations, they are likely to be deterred by the sheer size of the task. What is needed is some way of narrowing the field so that they and their parents can explore the occupation most likely to suit them. Job and training opportunities have changed markedly since parents made their own choices, so they should inform themselves of what is available. If the school has a careers library, you could ask to look through their literature.

'Well, I hope you learnt something here – remember it's not "Gissa job", it's "Have you any employment for me?" '
Reproduced by permission of *Punch*

Fortunately, many schools appoint a teacher to advise pupils in their choice of career. They have access to specialist and local information about jobs, and they may use vocational guidance tests. Dr Frederick Kuder, an American careers guidance specialist, has developed a preference questionnaire which measures interests in ten broad areas:

Outdoor: farming, land-surveyor, builder, gardener, etc.
Mechanical: mechanic, servicing equipment, engineer, etc.
Occupational: doctor, dentist, vet, accountant, psychologist, etc.
Scientific: scientist, laboratory technician, etc.
Persuasive: broadcaster, advertising agent, teacher, etc.
Artistic: artist, designer, window dresser, etc.
Literary: writer, journalist, etc.
Musical: musician, conductor, singer, music teacher, etc.
Social service: social worker, probation/parole officer, nurse, etc.
Clerical: secretary, clerk, etc.

The choice of occupation is indicated by an individual's preferences for certain types of activities. Different jobs have different *patterns* of interest associated with them; an extensive list of occupations that fit the major areas of interest is provided by Dr Kuder.

Another careers expert asks young people to list the occupations they have considered in thinking about their future, and then to list the careers they have daydreamed about and discussed with others. The answers to these questions and to a variety of questions about activities, competencies, occupations and estimates of themselves (on mechanical, scientific, artistic, teaching, sales, clerical, manual, mathematical, musical, friendship, managerial and office abilities) serve as 'occupation finders'.

Of course, there is a lot more to finding a job or vocation than assessing interests alone. Jobs make particular demands upon people's aptitudes; some of the main ones are listed below (with some of the occupations for which they would be crucial):

1 *Verbal ability*: verbal comprehension, the ability to understand written and spoken words (secretary, telephonist, teacher, shop assistant, copy-editor, etc.)

2 *Numeracy*: ability to understand and process numbers (banker, mathematician, accountant, cash till operator, computer systems analyst)

3 *Spatial ability*: ability to perceive and understand diagrams, objects, three- and two-dimensional shapes (surveyor, engineer, window dresser, artist, archaeologist)

4 *Originality*: creativity, originality in the use of words, numbers, shapes, pictures (architect, dress designer, artist, illustrator, producer/director, advertising agent, etc.)

5 *Word fluency*: the ability to be able to convey one's meaning clearly and vividly (journalist, broadcaster, salesperson, demonstrator, etc.)

6 *Memory*: remembering with ease, good retention and recall (solicitor, linguist, librarian, information officer, secretary, etc.)

7 *Perception*: ability to notice things in detail, (administrator, investment analyst, policeman, writer, cartographer)

8 *Reasoning*: good at working things out logically and clearly (scientist, work study officer, engineer, etc.)

A careers guidance expert will look not only at *single* aptitudes, but at the patterning of such abilities and their match with the teenager's interests, values (practicality, sociability, desire for security, attention, and so on), personal style (careful, dominant, dynamic, resilient, self-sufficient, and so on) and general health. The resultant profile should fit several occupations.

Further education

For many young people leaving school, opportunities are so varied that a wise choice can be made only on the basis of comprehensive, up-to-the-minute information. Some firms and organizations visit schools in order to provide firsthand information. Degree- and near-degree-level courses at polytechnics or colleges, or working while studying by day-release for a qualification, may suit some young people more than a university course.

For some adolescents a degree is vaguely perceived as a means to an end – a congenial job in business, the civil service, teaching, and so on. Some have a desire for a broad and liberal higher education without yet having a clear idea of what they want to do with it. Others have a clear vocation in mind and choose their course and university with great care, having a look at the relevant departments and talking to staff on their special visiting days.

As a marketable commodity, university degrees fall into two categories: first, an academic education which is not geared primarily to the business of training or earning a living; second, a course that is geared to provide students with a focused preparation for a vocation or career. Peter March and Michael Smith provide a flow chart (figure 4) as an aid to choosing a degree subject.

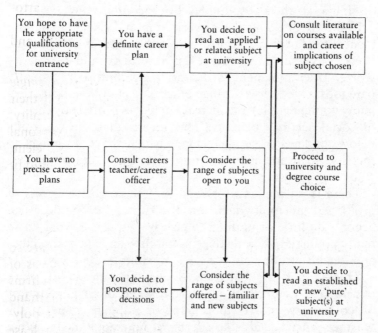

Figure 4   Choosing a university degree subject (from P. March and M. Smith (1977), Your Choice at 17+, *Cambridge: Hobson's Press)*

Unemployment

As many young people have become financially better off, their custom, as potential long-term bank savers and users, and as spenders on records, clothing, magazines and entertainment, has been assiduously solicited. Youth 'pop' culture has been cultivated in large part by commercial market forces. Self-esteem is explicitly related to material possessions. The mass advertising of goods and services for the affluent adolescent has dramatized the gap between the youthful 'haves' and 'have-nots' – a chasm steadily widening with the increase of unemployment among the young.

There is a risk, today, of growing numbers of young people who feel alienated and discriminated against. It is quite likely that young people's feelings of security and prosperity are related at least as much to their power to control their own destiny as to their absolute level of income.

In the UK the so-called poverty trap and rising unemployment (the latter an almost universal phenomenon in the West) have served to make both security and prosperity worse. Unemployment is demoralizing, but so are poorly paid jobs. Over a lower range of earnings (and this will affect many young people) any increase in wages is offset by the loss of social security benefits. This means that those earning below the level of supplementary benefit have no power to increase their income; the more they earn, the more they lose.

There is no panacea for reducing the corrosive effects of prolonged unemployment on the morale of adolescents. Schools do little or nothing to prepare pupils for what, in so many countries, is a distinct possibility and, in some cities and neighbourhoods in the UK, a distinct probability.

This is not the place to discuss the merits of work experience, Youth Training Schemes and other government or community efforts to prevent or mitigate some of the wastage and social side-effects of unemployment. What concerns parents is what to do about their son or daughter's hours of enforced leisure.

There are potential dangers in wait for those adolescents faced with a seemingly endless unstructured day, with only a succession of similarly boring days – without achievements, progress or hope – to look forward to. A large part of the problem is the unemployed person's inability to find things to do because of lack of money. It is not just a question of being unable to buy the clothes or records they would like. Unemployed youth cannot afford to go out as often to the cinema, disco or football match as their friends who are in work. Even going out for a drink can be prohibitively expensive, particularly when you may feel you must buy a round for six or seven people, for fear of appearing mean. Certain diversions might be sought with other young people in a similar plight. Excitement, especially adrenalin aroused by delinquent activity, is a marvellous antidote to depression and boredom. Drugs provide a temporary escape or 'analgesic' for some of them.

Another reaction leads to a more inward-directed problem – the development of what is called 'learned helplessness': a lack of desire to initiate actions, the adoption of a pessimistic view of life. What normally enhances teenagers' self-esteem and sense of competence, and immunizes them against fatalism, helplessness and depression, is the sense that their own actions play at least some part in controlling events. The danger is that long-unemployed adolescents may come to perceive events as being unrelated to their actions and thereby beyond personal control. Their lives (as they may be brought, by despair, to perceive them) are controlled by others, destiny, fate, chance – call it what you will.

How does one counteract such developments? The first consideration is how to attempt to bring some normality of 'structure' to the teenager's days. Some are quite likely to take to their beds, getting up at any hour of the day, or they succumb to the temptation to laze away the hours. The next call on your initiative and imagination is to suggest (or encourage your son or daughter to find) daily activities which bring about some sense of purpose and interest.

Surveys of problems experienced by youngsters in their

middle teens have confirmed that not being able to get a job is one of the main concerns of this age group. When occupational choice is denied the school-leaver, the opportunity to take part in other activities (social, economic, personal) vital to the development of a sense of personal identity may also be denied. One of the problems for the late adolescent could be that unemployment lengthens the stay within the parental home and prolongs dependence and what Erik Erikson calls the 'moratorium' – 'marking time' in the formation of identity.

Here, then, are clues for the enterprising parent. You need to counter the adverse effects of prolonged dependency by giving your son or daughter responsibility commensurate with their age and level of maturity. Is it possible to encourage and guide them into the kinds of activities and relationships with people that they would find at work? This is no problem if teenagers have a circle of friends. But they may lose friends and acquaintances after they leave school because of their dispersal to occupations elsewhere or distant colleges and universities.

A period of enforced leisure is a good time to educate oneself, to acquire skills in the arts or crafts. It could be a time to help others in a voluntary service or to initiate some enterprise to earn money. Advice on these matters is obtainable from various sources in the UK, notably regional advisory councils for further education, local authority social services, Citizens' Advice Bureaux or the local library.

The need to actively engage unemployment as a potential enemy is based upon hard evidence (not speculative rhetoric) about its ill-effects. There is evidence from a 1985 study by psychologist Dr A. Donovan that unemployed young people display a greater number of psychological symptoms (anxiety, depression, low self-esteem, physical malaise, antisocial behaviour, abuse of alcohol and drugs) than those in employment or those on government training schemes. The unemployed are much more likely to require professional psychological help than the employed. Whatever the details of what you do, the main thrust is to maintain a sense of normality in your teenagers' life. It is crucial that they face life, looking forward. It is only too easy to turn away from life by escaping from reality – as we shall see in the next chapter.

Chapter Seven

Alcohol and drug abuse

Drug use is now relatively common among adolescents, and drug abuse is a growing problem. But what are drugs? The term can be applied to many things from alcohol and cigarettes to cannabis and heroin. For the purposes of this chapter, however, we are talking specifically about drugs used illegally (such as cocaine, heroin and cannabis) and legal drugs (like alcohol and nicotine) whose use and misuse can exact awful penalties in the lives and wellbeing of individuals.

It is natural for parents to feel hurt and angry, and then desperate, when they discover that their child is taking drugs. But these emotions won't solve anything. However, knowledge about drugs and information on the expert advice available could help you to help your youngster or, better still, prevent a problem from getting started.

Teenagers do not know a world without cannabis and amphetamines, and it is not surprising if they are tempted to experiment a little. This does not make them addicts any more than getting drunk made their parents alcoholics when they were the same age. If someone takes a drug, it does not necessarily mean they will become addicted to it. Most young people are fairly sensible and not as unaware of the risks of excessive drug use as they are of excessive drinking.

However, some are inevitably at risk. They may take their first snort of heroin at a party and feel marvellous. Confident

The Department of Health and Social Security in England issues an excellent leaflet for parents, 'Drugs: what you can do as a parent' (DM4), on which some of the material in this chapter is based.

and relaxed, they feel daring, sophisticated and at one with their social group. This first experiment may be fun, and indeed so may the next; but somewhere along the line, early for some, later for others, comes the danger point, and for many the realization that they are hooked. The drug has assumed panacea properties which will solve all the problems of growing up and of living in a stressful environment. It is no longer an exciting experience, something to do for fun; it has become a crutch without which life is unsupportable. It functions in the same way as alcohol does for the alcoholic.

Almost all of us turn to drugs of one sort or another, at certain times, for pleasure and to help us relax. Alcohol and cigarettes are, of course, the most popular ones. But many of us also sometimes need drugs such as sleeping tablets, tranquillizers and antidepressants to help us ease our tensions and relieve our moods. Teenagers, it should be said, turn to their drugs for just the same reasons.

Cigarette smoking is a good example of these mixed motives: it has its pleasurable and its escapist components; it too can exact a heavy cost from those addicted to it. Teenagers who believe marijuana to be relatively harmless, as well as enjoyable, find it distinctly odd when parents who smoke cigarettes read the riot act to them about morality and health. Alcohol too offers an escape from unpleasant realities; it lifts the mood, reduces inhibition, erases tension and eases social intercourse; it offers moments of relief from worry and misery. Its misuse often leads to embarrassing drunken scenes, sexual indiscretions, brawls and even deaths on the roads. So what do we say to a teenager who tries drugs at a party? Adolescents are only too quick to spot hypocrisy in our self-righteous homilies.

Alcohol

Alcohol is as much a psychoactive drug as, say, marijuana. By that is meant that the person's subjective feelings and states of mind are altered by the effect of the drug on the central nervous system. The use, and abuse, of alcohol increases markedly during the adolescent years; in fact, there is a dramatic rise in drunkenness. Alcohol abuse is a far larger problem among juveniles in the UK than the abuse of drugs. Pubs and bars cater increasingly for young people, and today drinking is very much part of their life, just as it always has been for various groups of adults. In the USA drugs are more likely to loom in the consciousness of parents or school and welfare authorities responsible for children and adolescents.

Interestingly, the early use of alcohol is correlated with the use of illicit drugs. There is a well-documented sequence; almost no adolescent who uses hard drugs has not already used alcohol, tobacco and marijuana. This does not, of course, mean that adolescents who smoke and then drink *necessarily* go on to use marijuana or try hard drugs.

Most adult alcoholism begins with excessive drinking in adolescence. Those teenagers tend to have problems in coping with their impulsiveness and aggression; males often overemphasize their masculinity and underemphasize (or deny) their dependency and anxiety. Some display behaviour problems and delinquent actions. The excessive drinker seems to be the sort of youngster who has a particular need for power; drinking enhances and assuages this feeling of, and craving for, power. Family influences, as usual, play their part. They *predispose* the offspring to alcohol abuse. One often finds heavy drinking among the teenager's family, notably the father.

It is worth pausing here to pursue this notion of pre-disposition; it is a particularly important concept in the causation of this and other complex psychological disorders.

There are different levels at which one can explain (or interpret) actions. The adolescent's liability to behave in a particular manner at a particular time is determined by a variety of *contributory influences* (general predisposing factors which set the stage for particular actions) and a series of *causes* (specific events which directly elicit and maintain behaviours of one kind or another).

A child who (for whatever reason) suffers from low morale and depression, exposed to the continuous example of an admired, hard-drinking, 'try anything' older brother, might well be predisposed to use alcohol inappropriately. Whether the precipitating cause will come into action depends on various other factors. The behaviour may be triggered by a dare from friends, or an easy opportunity to drink alcohol at a party. After the first step in drinking, the habit may cease immediately or in the not too distant future. If the act of drinking is reinforced by the approval of friends, by the good feelings experienced, and the feeling that he or she has got away with it despite being under age, repetition may lead to habitual drinking. Whether it will be appropriate social drinking or excessive, compulsive drinking will depend on further predisposing and circumstantial factors.

We have seen that adolescence can be a difficult time for some young people: those who are under pressure at school, those who are on bad terms with their parents or no terms at all with their peers. For some, work, or the lack of work, is frustrating and boring. All of this means *temptation* when an acquaintance offers an unhappy youngster something which is 'fun', something which everyone else is taking. Many children say no; a growing number appease their curiosity or give in to the social pressure.

Not all of those who use alcohol or other drugs can be said to be unhappy, emotionally disturbed or psychiatrically vulnerable. Most youngsters will outgrow drugs and the drug scene. The risk for some is that of becoming addicted accidentally, because the dangers have not been fully assesed, hence the importance of education about drugs. What may begin as a fairly harmless experimenting with various substances for pleasure may, when the drug is addictive (i.e. when tolerance increases rapidly with time), become a dependency. Such a person's unwitting slide into dependency differs from the depressed, inadequate-feeling youngster, who eagerly embraces the 'lift' or 'anaesthetic' quality of drugs.

Although we cannot change an adolescent's past, we may be able to release him or her from the tyranny of history in so far as it sours present attitudes or clouds day-to-day judgements. The most effective help lies in helping adolescents to deal with the current circumstances surrounding their drinking.

The psychologist John Travers (in his 1977 study) is of the opinion that the most difficult decision for the teenager is not whether to drink or to abstain. The real conundrum is *how* to live with his or her decision, whichever way it goes. He offers parents the following guidelines to give to their teenagers:

1 Whatever you decide, know the positive reasons for your decision. If we have said you're too young to begin drinking, or you dislike the taste, treat these as valid and honest reasons for your decision.
2 There is no need to apologize for your decision. Others should respect your decision to abstain. (If they don't, is their opinion worthy of respect?)
3 Respect, in turn, *their* decision to drink, even if you disagree with it.
4 If you decide to drink, obey the laws on drinking.
5 Use alcohol; don't abuse it. Do not drink to excess in order to appear sophisticated. Do not drink and drive.
6 Learn how to take alcohol moderately by observing those who enjoy one or two drinks in order to relax, to socialize and to accompany their food.
7 Notice how they drink or sip slowly and space their drinks.

Remember to tread carefully when talking to your son or daughter about alcohol or other drugs. A wrong word at the wrong time can edge them into rebellion and you achieve the opposite of what you hoped for. But the right word of understanding can strengthen latent decisions *not* to take a drink or try a drug.

Drug misuse and abuse

A drug is loosely defined as any substance which exerts a chemical action on the body, and which is not required for ordinary nourishment. In this context, I refer specifically to those substances which exert some action on the mental state. There are several main groups of this kind. They are described in table 3, along with their risks and consequences.

The terms 'drug abuse' and 'drug misuse' refer to the observation that a particular form of drug-taking is a harmful (abuse) and/or socially unacceptable way of using that substance (misuse). 'Users' – as people who take drugs usually refer to themselves – are likely to develop 'tolerance' for a drug, which means that their body has adapted to the repeated presence of the drug so that *higher* doses are required to maintain the same effect. The body may react with 'withdrawal effects' to the sudden absence of a drug to which it has adapted; they involve severe physical discomfort. When this occurs and leads to a compulsion to continue taking the drug so as to avoid these symptoms, we speak of 'physical dependence'. The more important and widespread problem is called 'psychological dependence', and this refers to an irresistible psychological compulsion to repeat the stimulation, pleasure or comfort provided by the drug's effects.

Physical withdrawal symptoms used to be the criterion for designating a drug as addictive, but *psychological* dependence appears more crucial to addiction than physical dependence. In fact the term 'addiction' is in some disrepute; although the term has been used at different times and by various practitioners as a diagnostic label for drug and substance abuse, it has resisted any precise definition about which experts can agree.

Many people use drugs without coming to harm, but there are very serious dangers. The Institute for the Study of Drug Dependence, in Britain, lists them as follows:

1 *Overdoing it.*
(a) Taking too much at one go could lead to a fatal overdose or an extremely distressing experience.
(b) Taking high doses frequently may impair mental and physical functioning and normal development.
(c) Financing drug purchase can lead to a deterioration of

Table 3 *Abuse potential of different classes of drugs: risks and consequences*

	Opioids[a]	Sedatives[a]	Tranquillizers[b]	Stimulants[c]	Hallucinogens[d]	Cannabis[e]	Inhalants	Cocaine	Alcohol
Acute intoxication leading to life-threatening overdose	yes	yes	possible (esp. if taken with alcohol)	possible	rare	none documented	yes	yes	yes
Relative potential for dependence/addiction	high	moderate to high	low	high	low	low to moderate	low	high	moderate
Risk of progressive organ damage, possibly irreversible	low[f]	low to moderate	low	moderate	low	low	high	moderate	high
'Flashbacks'	no	no	no	no	yes	yes	no	no	no
'Panic reactions' (acute toxic psychosis)	no	no	no	yes	yes	yes	no	yes	no

	a	b	c	d	e	f	
Persistent psychotic reaction	no	yes	possible	yes	possible	possible	possible	yes
Risk of serious social dysfunction or 'life-style consequences'	very high	high	low	low to moderate	low to moderate	low to moderate	very high	moderate to high
Organic brain syndrome (severe or long-lasting adverse mental or behavioural consequences)	low to moderate	moderate	low	moderate to high	high	low	high	moderate to high

a   Barbiturates, chlormethiazole and other 'neo-barbiturates'.
b   Valium, Tranxene, Ativan, etc.
c   Amphetamines and related stimulants (e.g. Preludin, Ritalin).
d   LSD, mescaline, 'mushrooms', DOM, DOB, MDA, MDM, etc.
e   Marijuana and other cannabis derivatives such as hashish and hash oil.
f   Low organ damage assumes the drug is given in a pure, known dosage form under sterile conditions to otherwise healthy individuals.

Source: I. Mothner and A. Weitz (1986), *How to Get Off Drugs* (Harmondsworth: Penguin)

diet and housing, and the degradation of a person's lifestyle.

2 *Wrong time, wrong place.* In moderate doses most psychoactive drugs impair attention, reaction time and motor co-ordination, thus affecting driving, operating machinery, studying, and other activities.

3 *Adulteration and mistaken identity.* Drugs offered on the illicit market are not always what they are claimed to be. They are likely to contain impurities and adulterants with unpredictable, possibly dangerous effects.

4 *Doubling up.* Doubling up drugs, loading one drug on top of another, multiplies the risks of a harmful outcome. Some users take several drugs; complex interactions can occur which may prove fatal.

5 *Injection.* This is the most hazardous method of taking drugs (opiates, sedatives and stimulants), but is fortunately not as widespread as other ways of taking them. The major dangers are from overdose, infections (e.g. hepatitis, AIDS), abscesses and gangrene.

6 *Pregnancy.* The foetus can be damaged by drug use in the pregnant mother.

7 *Drug laws.* The user and supplier of drugs are at risk by breaking drug laws which are very wide; penalties, too, can be very heavy.

8 *Individual differences.* Drug effects vary with individual's body weight and psychological make-up. The young person who is likely to become addicted is very often the same kind of individual who is at risk of serious mental illness in late adolescence, and the same sort of background tends to be common to both: a broken home, parental strife, and a dominating or ineffective mother or father – parents who provide little by way of example or standards. It is, in fact, quite exceptional to come across a young person addicted to drugs who has not had quite severe family problems. That is not to say that these problems are the

actual *cause* of addiction, but rather that drug-taking is one of a number of ways of dealing with apparently intractable personal problems, a peculiarly contemporary way.

The exposure to drug-taking is more pervasive than mere personal contact and example. Part of the difficulty of being moralistic about the subject in relation to teenagers is that we, as adults, live in a drug-orientated society. Countless sedatives, tranquillizers and antidepressants are prescribed by doctors to help 'make life easier'.

We can be addicted to, or dependent upon, many other things than drugs. It is probably more fruitful to refer to drug 'use' rather than drug addiction. If we knew more about safe substance *use* (e.g. appropriate or acceptable alcohol use), we would be in a better position to consider calmly and objectively the issues of substance *abuse*, as it affects individuals and their community.

Drug abuse is *relatively* infrequent among schoolchildren, but not as rare as it used to be; it becomes more common during the years of adolescence. Fortunately, most youngsters who try drugs out of curiosity do not continue to use them regularly. Those who take drugs tend to do so infrequently and give them up altogether after a year or so.

The key factor in drug-taking is opportunity – the availability of drugs and people to tempt and 'prompt'. Users have generally been exposed to drugs by their peers or by people (not infrequently family members) whose values incline towards nonconformity or even deviance. Rebelliousness, low self-esteem, a poor sense of psychological wellbeing (including depression) and low academic aspirations are among characteristics commonly found in adolescent drug users. The boredom and hopelessness of unemployment also play their part.

High-risk drug-taking is defined as uncontrolled use, whether or not it is already demonstrably harmful. A person is also taking an unacceptable risk if he or she is a *regular* user, that is to say taking drugs at predictable intervals. Low-risk usage, not surprisingly, is much more difficult to specify. Ira Mothner and Alan Weitz, the authors of a helpful book

How to Get Off Drugs, maintain that, while the occasional use, in a social or intimate setting, of a substance such as cannabis would seem to be a low-risk activity, there are people whose sensitivity to the drug is so great that even this involvement is very risky. Nevertheless, for large numbers of users, the occasional social use is within the low-risk range. The difficulty, they say, is keeping it there, and preventing oneself from gradually increasing the dosage or finding more opportunities to use drugs, thus beginning a slow slide towards comprehensive use.

The motives for seriously using drugs in the long term are many and varied. There may be an element of defiance in it, doing what the parents disapprove of and fear; there may be a special attraction if the adolescent knows that this is something the parents have never experienced. There is pressure to conform in experiencing new sensations and sharing them with other members of one's own age group. The elements of risk and excitement certainly exert a strong pull towards experimenting with drugs. But, however much these various factors may contribute to the decision to take drugs, the chief motive for a great many teenagers is their wish to escape from precisely those problems which make adolescence, for them, such a difficult and stressful period of life.

Perhaps we should not be too surprised that disadvantaged adolescents – looking to a future with little hope and facing economic, social and racial discrimination, enduring degrading living conditions, often with untreated physical ills, suffering disintegration in their social environment and in their own families – give up the search for meaning and personal identity, and seek escape in the oblivion of narcotics.

As I explained in chapter 1, individuals acquire, over long periods of time, strategies for dealing or simply coping with situations they consider to be depressing, dangerous or threatening. There are also (it is argued) three basic types of self-protective response. They have evolved from basic *biological* defensive mechanisms – attack, submission and flight – which are still useful, but were of greater utility to our ancestors who lived and hunted in close proximity to a variety of animal predators. When used to excess by an individual they become self-defeating. Flight is the motivating factor at work in many cases of drug abuse. This method of coping in life involves strategic withdrawal, and takes the form of psychological retreat such as escape or avoidance behaviour, inhibition or emotional insulation.

There is a tendency to think 'It couldn't happen to me – I'm different.' But nobody is so different as to be completely invulnerable, beyond risk. Having said that, there are certainly people who have a greater tolerance of frustration, anxiety and stress than their fellows.

To have recourse to drugs when worried, depressed or insecure does not bring any solution to adolescent problems. Rather it serves to deny them, if only temporarily; the escape route is illusory and can lead to worse problems – drugs as an all-consuming way of life.

Stimulants and sedatives

Although the effects of amphetamines ('speed') on a teenager seem harmless at first, they are dangerous in that they lead to habit formation. The first important danger sign is the development of tolerance, when there is a need to increase the dose to achieve the desired effect. Teenagers who take pills such as amphetamines may feel they are learning better; but tests show there is actually very little benefit, and in some cases learning ability is even impaired. Athletes, on the other hand, definitely perform better, and allegations of 'doping' usually concern this type of drug.

Under the influence of amphetamines, people look bright and are more than usually talkative. When large quantities have been taken, users may be irritable, restless and unable to sleep, and in extreme cases there may be severe mental disorder, with fantasies of persecution and frightening visions.

Sedatives, designed to 'bring people down' or to 'take the

edge off' difficulties, are best represented by the barbiturates. Addiction here is very hard to reverse.

Solvent abuse

There is nothing new about the inhalation of solvents. A variety of substances were used in this way in ancient times, to bring about euphoria, hallucinations, relief from tension and to achieve states of altered consciousness. Solvent abuse by young people (especially glue-sniffing) has received a lot of publicity of late, but has been quite widespread since the 1940s. Glues, nail polish and remover, petrol, paint, dry-cleaning compounds and a variety of aerosols are just a few of the solvents put to such dangerous use – being inhaled in paper and plastic bags, or sniffed directly from containers or sprays.

The physical manifestations of such activities can be recognized from the discolorations and marks that appear on the face or other parts of the bodies. Solvent abusers do not fit into any neat category of personality type. But many show very low self-esteem, notably those who do not give up after a short period of experimentation. Those who continue the habit as loners have a worse outlook than those who abuse solvents with others as a group activity. They usually have a disrupted, stressful family background that includes marital discord. Escape from harsh reality is yet again the rationale for this kind of abuse.

Cannabis

This is a mild hallucinogenic drug; it can be grown almost anywhere. It has many hundreds of names in local slang, the best known being *hash* or *hashish*, *marijuana*, *grass*, *pot*, *dope* or *charge*. It has been known for thousands of years and its use is really widespread.

Cannabis is, in fact, second only to alcohol as the world's most popular drug of abuse. It is widely used in the UK and USA, is easily available, and is smoked often, to enhance already enjoyable activities like parties, pop festivals and sex. It is usually smoked mixed in with tobacco in a roll-your-own cigarette, and produces a characteristic sweetish smell. It has a disinhibiting effect which makes the smoker feel pleasantly high. Cannabis smokers claim that there is no harm in the habit, or at least that it is no more harmful than tobacco or alcohol, and that the legal restrictions which have been put upon its use are unnecessary.

According to Mothner and Weitz, cannabis (like cocaine) seems to have a better name than it deserves. They make the point that most smokers appear to suffer little for their enjoyment, but the evidence suggests that it is a high-risk drug for *certain users*: pregnant women, nursing mothers, anyone with a respiratory or heart problem, epileptics and (worrying in this context) adolescents. The evidence of long-term effects, and the risks they may pose for all users, has been of fairly recent origin.

The drug can produce tolerance, and long-term use may lead to psychological dependency, if not (and this is debatable) physical dependency. It is what is called a 'gateway' drug; although smoking joints will *not* necessarily lead to heroin use, most addicts do seem to get started with cannabis before escalating to the more powerful drugs. It stands somewhere between its 1930s reputation for being a public menace (together with its 1960s reputation of leading directly to heroin addiction) and its more recent aura of being wholly benign and completely harmless.

The drug engenders a sense of wellbeing, during which thoughts and feelings can seem vivid and more meaningful, time and space tend to be distorted, fine judgement may be lost and emotional feelings exaggerated. It is said to be hard to give up. It is suggested that, as with other drugs, those most likely to take it (and the differences are particularly marked in adolescence) are those already unhappy, suffering from anxiety or depression, low self-esteem and low expectations, or trying to escape from the realities of life. Dr Stephen Pittel, an American specialist who has investigated drug effects and treatment for nearly two decades, writes that young people 'tend to turn to marijuana during adolescence because they haven't developed the internal resources to deal with adolescence'. In this sense it is potentially dangerous for teenagers if it gets in the way of realistic solutions to problems.

LSD, heroin and cocaine

LSD (lysergic acid diethylamide) became widely used in the 1960s when it was the main hallucinogenic drug taken by those seeking mystical experiences, but there are numerous other substances, mostly from plants in Central and South America, which may bring on similar visions in susceptible people. LSD produces similar reactions to cannabis, only in exaggerated form. It is one of the most powerful substances known.

Heroin ('smack', 'skag') is one of the opiates, which also includes opium and derivates of it, such as morphine, thebaine and codeine. Until about 100 years ago, opium, or laudanum, was just about the most useful drug in a doctor's medicine bag. Even now, these drugs are unique in relieving pain and inducing a sense of wellbeing.

It is generally inhaled (from the fumes of the powder heated on silver foil) or injected into a vein (a method known as 'mainlining'); the effects come on fairly quickly and are highly addictive. Feelings of peace, detachment and 'clouding' are described by addicts, but the main pleasure of a heroin injection is that it brings sheer relief to a pervasive, compulsive craving which torments the longstanding user.

During the 'high' period lasting three to four hours, users have a faraway look; they do not want to be disturbed and resent noise and bright light. The most important outward sign is that the pupils become very small. A 'level' period of another four hours follows, in which addicts appear more or less normal, and this is the time when they can go out and about. Eight hours or so after the injection, they are likely to need another 'fix', and they then become progressively more agitated and irritable, unable to concentrate. The full-blown withdrawal state develops if no heroin or substitute drug is given.

Like most of the other drugs, heroin has no directly damaging action on the body, in the sense that alcohol damages the liver, the brain or the heart. However, a young heroin addict is nearly thirty times more likely to die within the succeeding year than a non-addict. Death often results from suicide, accidental overdose, undernourishment, or infection from unsterilized syringes. Half of today's heroin addicts will be dead before they reach the end of their twenties.

Cocaine ('coke') is a drug which has insinuated itself into all levels of American society, and which is fast gaining popularity in Britain. Compared to heroin it is an expensive drug. There are debates about whether it creates physical dependency, but it certainly causes psychological dependency; it is considered a very dangerous drug and particularly difficult to deal with.

Cocaine is produced from a shrub which flowers high on the eastern slopes of the Andes. It is a brief-acting stimulant that works on the central nervous system and is a potent local anaesthetic. What some users get from cocaine is relief from depression; other seek its help in improving their performance at work, socializing or during sex. Confidence is boosted, wellbeing is enhanced and problems diminish. If offers euphoria quickly, but its effects soon dissipate, within half-an-hour to an hour. That 'high' is powerfully reinforcing – more so probably than any other psychoactive drug. Cocaine is sniffed, smoked, swallowed or injected.

The regular use of cocaine, like *any* other drug, exacts its price. It leads to many adverse effects: restlessness, irritability, apprehension, suspicion and sometimes paranoid symptoms (extreme suspiciousness, persecutory feelings) being common. Intravenous injections ('mainlining') result, when the 'high' is over, in a profound depression (the 'crash'). Snorting (sniffing) cocaine damages the nasal passages. The main risks to health come from overdosing (which may be fatal), from anorexia, from the use of unsterilized syringes, and from lung and liver damage.

If you should find yourself in an emergency where a boy or girl has overdosed and is unconscious or drowsy, take the following steps:

1 First make certain they have fresh air.
2 Turn them on their side, and try not to leave them alone (otherwise they could inhale vomit).
3 Telephone for a doctor or ambulance.
4 Collect any tablets, powders, etc., and take them to the hospital for examination.

Helping and preventing drug dependency

It is most important for parents and teachers to be on the lookout for signs that may lead them to suspect drug use. It isn't easy, because some of the signs are not uncommon in adolescence generally. There is often a gradual change in the adolescent's habits and a general lethargy. Other signs include sudden changes of mood; uncharacteristic irritability or aggression; loss of interest in school work, sport, hobbies and friends; furtive behaviour and frequent lying; bouts of drowsiness or sleeplessness; unexplained disappearances of money and belongings from the home.

Heroin addicts usually stop bothering about their appearance, their speech may become halting, and they tend to drop old friends and take up with new ones. Users of heroin may receive unexplained messages or telephone calls, followed by an immediate and unexplained departure. Spots of blood may be noticed on their clothes, and (most important) needle marks on the back of the hand and the inside of the elbow. There may also be thickened brownish cords under the skin, which are veins, solidified as a result of the injections. The addict has little interest in sex or in human relationships. There is a tendency to be hostile to society, and therein lies part of the trouble when it comes to treatment and rehabilitation.

A hospital too often epitomizes society in the mind of the

addict. More informal methods are therefore required, and in most countries clinics run on 'non-institutional' lines within the community, and more casual in style, are being set up. Sadly such agencies and local drug advice centres are thin on the ground in the UK. Most promising, however, seem to be those communities which are run by ex-addicts. The addict who is desperate for drugs has an uncanny instinct for putting the most subtle and painful pressures on families and doctors alike, but these tactics are familiar to ex-addicts and therefore get nowhere with them.

If you want confidential advice, contact your doctor, a social worker or Citizens' Advice Bureau for names and addresses of local services. There are self-help groups which exist to support concerned parents. In the UK you can dial 100 and ask for Freefone 'Drug Problems' for information about local drug advice centres.

Ira Mothner and Alan Weitz provide a checklist of questions that adult users should ask themselves about their drug use and its impact on their lives. This may be helpful to parents or teachers in assessing the dependency of teenagers in their care. Questions on drug use are:

1 Do you use drugs when you are alone?
2 Can you turn down a joint or a line of coke if it is offered?
3 Do you get high before seeing non-using friends?
4 Do you need *something* (a joint, a tranquillizer or something stronger) before going to sleep?
5 Do you ever take something (a drink, a joint, a stimulant) first thing in the morning?
6 Do you feel flat and dull when you are not using?
7 How large a supply do you keep, and how concerned do you become when you start to run out?
8 Can you get through a full day without drugs and feel no distress?
9 Is it becoming difficult to pay for all the drugs you want?

Questions on the impact of drugs are:

1 Do you have many non-using friends?

2 How many of your drug friends would you want to keep if you stopped using?
3 Is there more friction in your dealings with colleagues and co-workers than before you used drugs?
4 Is your boss (teacher) less interested in your work?
5 If you are at school or university is your work suffering?
6 Did you get the last pay increase you thought you deserved?
7 Do you have less patience for detail and find it harder to master new material?
8 Do you often find yourself rereading the same page?
9 Are there times when you lose track of conversations?
10 Do you believe sex is better when you are high?
11 Are you sexually aroused less frequently?
12 Are you capable of an erection, an orgasm?
13 Are you interested in sustaining a relationship?
14 Do you feel you give as much as your partner to your marriage or relationship?
15 How does he or she feel about your drug use and your relationship?

The wrong answers are obvious, and anyone should raise questions about how much control the user has over his or her drug use and how much life is being adversely affected. The authors make the point that, whoever the drug user is or what kind of drugs he or she has used, there will be the same four steps to be taken in coming off the treadmill.

1 Recognize that you have a problem and decide to do something about it.
2 Give up, and go through whatever withdrawal is involved.
3 Make the changes in your life that will enable you to remain drug-free.
4 Cope with whatever problems subsequently arise.

In the American and British editions of this book there are addresses of the varied services available to assist drug users in their rehabilitation.

It is vital for the user who has come off drugs to be active, to find new activities and social networks (away from the drug-user circuit). Studies indicate that former drug users who relocate themselves were many more times successful in remaining abstinent than those who remained in the same place.

Prevention of drug abuse is, of course, the best way of helping. Shock tactics, such as horror stories about the dangers of smoking, drinking or drug-taking, have not proved effective as deterrents; in fact they can be counter-productive. Calm, objective education is more likely to forewarn teenagers of the risks. The school – with its access to so many young people – seems an obvious place to inform them about drugs and, by providing accurate information, meet their natural curiosity about the subject. It must not be an amateurish *ad hoc* business. Any educational programme requires skilful teachers and a sophisticated curriculum.

One benefit of drug education programmess, whether or not they prevent drug use (and the evidence is far from complete), may be to make young people more cautious and discriminating in their choice of drugs. An increased aware-ness in adolescents of the dangers of LSD might explain the decline of the LSD fashion.

Several lines of research into the effectiveness of educa-tional programmes (and notably the 1980s work of the British Institute for the Study of Drug Dependence) suggest some guidelines:

1 Avoid exaggerated statements about drugs. The Insti-tute's survey showed that a sizeable proportion of pupils knew, at first hand, a drug-taker. So teenagers may be able to compare melodramatic or inaccurate claims (e.g. 'Cannabis damages the brain' or 'Cannabis *always* leads to heroin') with real-life knowledge; your views and words (of serious intent) might thus be devalued.

2 It is essential for teachers on educational programmes to determine the pupils' beliefs and attitudes to drugs *before* deciding to introduce any distinctive programme of drug education. A key factor is the existing level of familiarity with

drugs. The more familiar pupils are with drugs, the more likely they are to reject anti-drug claims made in the lessons.

3 Lessons which aim *broadly* at prevention are likely to be less effective than lessons with more modest objectives.

4 The teacher's limited objectives could include:
(a) reducing the likelihood of experimentation with a particular drug;
(b) promotion of a particular attitude to drugs;
(c) clarifying the reasons (e.g. the difficulty of saying no when with friends) which might lead to acceptance of drugs in a particular situation.

5 It is very important to obtain feedback on the effects of drug education lessons, whether through individual discussions, written work or evaluated research. The information gained can be used to modify subsequent teaching.

6 Do not be misled by immediate impressions. Immediate effects of drug education programmes are a poor guide to long-term effects.

Chapter Eight

Problems in the school

Mass formal education has created serious problems for life goals for adolescents with education disabilities. For academically successful adolescents, school is a bridge between the world of childhood and the world of adulthood. For children unwilling or unable to learn, school is a place where the battle against society is likely to begin.

(Professor S. Toby)

Educational success and failure

The academic demands made of children and adolescents are greater today than ever before. There is little doubt that standards of educational attainment, in the population as a whole, are much higher than they were even a generation ago.

What should make us reflect about the educational system are the large numbers of young people who do well, or reasonably well, in life's business both prior to and after the school years, but who during those years – for a variety of reasons – are judged to be incompetent or poorly 'adjusted'. For many children who have been condemned at school, the great release comes when they go out into the adult world and have to earn a living and perhaps support a family. They find new incentives and rewards for their efforts, and they surprise themselves with the capacity for hard work and application which they discover with pleasure that they possess.

There are teenagers, in increasing numbers today, who

may do well at school, but whose hopes are blighted by a lack of opportunities and employment in the outside world. School does not prepare them for long periods of involuntary 'leisure' and the demoralizing status of being unemployed. Being employed (or underemployed) in symbolic, artificially created jobs is small comfort for enterprising young people.

The pressure for success and for 'results' in our competitive society is enormous; the price of failure is a heavy one. To mention the words 'academic success' in some circles is to generate a heated debate. Some schools are criticized for their tunnel vision of success, based upon a narrowly conceived and exam-orientated curriculum.

But social status – rightly or wrongly – depends to a large degree on occupation. Occupation, in turn, is associated very much with academic qualifications. If academic success is going to be measured in terms of the social status to which it opens doors, then the main criteria are likely to involve the level, grade and number of formal qualifications obtained by the student. Inevitably, however, competition, selectivity and discrimination enter the educational equation, much to the concern of many parents, children and, indeed, educationists.

The headmaster of a large British secondary school, Bernard Barker, writes that some of the early 1980s schools have had to face the truth that examination success and competition lead nowhere for many young people. He says that teachers have recognized that their task is to enable *all* children to participate in society and to organize activities through which everyone can develop varied skills. Opportunity and streaming (separating children by their abilities) are not enough now, in his opinion. Academic disciplines no longer define the curriculum; subjects are interpreted through their interrelationship. No lesson is considered simply practical or theoretical; it is well understood that all learning requires both practical experiment and a developing understanding of the concepts. Teachers believe that students should experience a wide range of topics, whatever their ability or future employment destination. Barker concludes that citizenship depends upon a broad understanding of man and nature; schools prefer to be architects of democracy rather than transmit merely useful knowledge.

But schools are a microcosm of the society they serve. No matter how good they are, they can only do so much for the young people who have been severely disadvantaged or damaged by the circumstances of their lives – sometimes from the time of their birth onwards. These children are programmed for failure, unless the opportunity arises to disrupt or remedy pernicious influences.

Failure in a success-orientated world has significant consequences for the wellbeing of adolescents, not only at school, but in other facets of their lives. There is a strong association between emotional disturbance and under-achievement at school – a perennial matter of concern to both teachers and parents. Emotionally disturbed adolescents tend to distract and harass their teachers, and disrupt and anger their more conscientious fellow students.

A sense of failure very often manifests itself in an obstinate façade behind which the student hides. There is a vicious circle of self-fulfilling prophecy at work. Tell teenagers often enough that they are fools, criticize them whatever they do, even if it is commendable within their own capabilities, and in the end they will become extremely demoralized and even give up. Why should they work hard when all their efforts, good and bad, are condemned? Their confidence will be destroyed and once again they may retreat behind a mask of stupidity and 'don't care' laziness.

Young people who do well at school tend to enjoy good health, have average or above-average intelligence and well-developed social skills. They are likely to have a good opinion of themselves, the ability to gauge accurately their effect on others, and to perceive correctly the quality of others' approaches and responses to themselves. Early-maturing boys and girls have many advantages in terms of capability and self-confidence.

All of this begs the question: what is success? It is surely inadequate to judge academic success solely by means of eductional criteria (such as exams) which largely determine occupational status. Many other advantages are provided by schools – personal relationships, social skills and attitudes – and these too may have a marked influence on people's careers. Academic success might also be defined by psychological criteria, in terms of the acquisition of certain kinds of experience – incentive, knowledge and intellectual skills outside the relatively narrow confines of the examination curriculum. Success does involve more than attainment; it involves curiosity about the world, the opening of minds, the motivation to *use* and capitalize on one's education.

Some young people have the right raw material to attain reasonable standards in our achievement-geared society, but for a variety of reasons don't do so. They are called 'under-achievers'. The under-achiever's academic performance is significantly below that predicted on the basis of a measure of intelligence or scholastic aptitude. Chronic under-achievement in boys of above-average aptitude may begin in the primary school. It is not so likely to show itself in girls until they reach secondary school. Adolescents who fail at school may be of lower than average IQ, but intellectually well-endowed young people can also do poorly.

There is broadly speaking a correlation between IQ and educational achievement. Parents often ask about the development of intelligence at adolescence. The problem is that no definitive statement can be made about the nature of intelligence. To begin with, it is a multi-faceted phenomenon; intellectual activity takes many forms. It is not a thing, an entity in the mind; rather, it is an abstract concept which psychologists have found useful to summarize many mental activities which underlie behaviour we choose to call 'intelligent' or 'unintelligent' in everyday life. Intelligence is a collection of abilities. We talk of verbal intelligence, a facility with words and verbal problems; and spatial intelligence, a facility with spatial relationships, and so on.

Psychologists measure intelligence by administering standardized tests of mental ability to individuals and estimating from their scores their intellectual ability relative to other people of the same age. The IQ (intelligence quotient) is an index of the relationship. They divide intelligence into two kinds; the first being 'fluid ability', an unspecialized type which involves abstract thinking and reveals itself in new situations where successful adaptation cannot rely on the person's existing repertoire of intellectual skills. This ability reaches its maximum growth at adolescence. The subsequent decline is not noticeable until after the age of about 25. The other type, sometimes referred to as 'crystallized ability' or 'verbal and educational ability', refers to the intelligence which allows the individual to assimilate and learn from new experiences. Crystallized intelligence reveals itself in those tests which require learned habits of thinking. This ability may continue to develop (particularly in the individual who uses his or her mind) throughout adult life.

IQ is *not* the only thing that matters. Other attributes, such as motivation, persistence and wisdom, are also critical factors. Most under-achievers fail to find academic work rewarding, and, when they do work, they exert little effort. They are easy to distract, seldom complete their work, and set themselves low standards of academic achievement. Under-achievers generally find school unsatisfying, and develop negative attitudes towards teachers. There may be faults in the school and the school system, but we must not be too quick to use them as scapegoats. That would be too facile; we need to look at the youngster, the school and the home environment.

A critical problem for teachers is how to boost the adolescent's attainment at school by giving him or her access to some of the success we all wish to enjoy. A behavioural method called 'shaping' could be helpful. Shaping involves the use of reinforcement (see chapter 10) and a shifting criterion of success.

In order to encourage pupils to behave (or perform a skill) in a way they have never done before, the teacher works out the successive steps they must take so as to approximate more and more closely to the desired final outcome. This process, called 'shaping' or the principle of 'successive approximations', involves taking mini-steps towards the final goal. The teacher begins by reinforcing very small changes in performance which are in the right direction, even if still far removed from the final desired outcome. No reinforcement is given for performance in the 'wrong' direction. Gradually the criteria of the individual's approximation to the desired goal are made more rigorous. It is crucial to begin at a level at which the pupil will experience success.

It is possible to summarize the factors that enhance (or disrupt) successful attainment at school as follows:

1 the interest, encouragement and aspirations of parents;
2 the nature and amount of formal education parents received;
3 the cultural interests and reading habits of parents;
4 the size of the family – children from large families tending to do less well;
5 birth order – eldest children, on average, are more achievement-orientated;
6 the quality of maternal care – the development of reading skills is particularly affected by positive factors in this area;
7 poverty, which adversely influences attainment;
8 factors associated with social disorganization (high rates of illegitimacy, birth, crime, neglect of children, etc.) which are, in turn, associated with low attainment;
9 disruption of family life – such as broken homes – which affects attainment adversely, particularly in middle-class children.

Authoritative parents are most likely to facilitate the development of competence and self-reliance in young children by enhancing responsible, purposive and independent behaviour. The psychologist, David McClelland, who has devoted many years to research on influences on motivation and achievement in America, maintains that what is desirable is an emphasis on the child meeting certain achievement standards between the ages of 6 and 8. The young person, later on in development, is likely to be highly motivated if, in addition, he or she is held in warm regard by both parents, who are ambitious for their offspring but not too dominating, and who have a strong, positive attitude towards education.

There can be little doubt that hereditary factors are also a major source of individual differences in attainment. Environmental factors too can enhance, stunt or distort attainment. Social-class differences in attainment increase as children grow older. A study by J. W. B. Douglas and colleagues (1968) of a large random sample of all children born in Britain in one week in 1946 found that differences between the average attainments of the offspring of manual and non-manual workers increased between the ages of 8 and 11. Irrespective of the level of attainment, significant differences appeared at age 11 between children of the two classes who *had been equal* at age 8.

Social class is also closely related to school-leaving age; according to the 'Youth in Transition' study, working-class children in the USA are less likely to stay on at school for a sixth-year course. By the age of 18 more than half of those who had left school early had failed at least one grade in school, compared to only 27 per cent of the high school graduates. Students gave as their reasons for dropping out statements which were consistent with low academic ability. As one put it, 'I was mostly just discouraged because I wasn't passing.' Students who were lower in academic ability, as measured by the standardized tests of ability, were more likely to drop out.

Students in the 'Youth in Transition' study were given a personality test to measure what is called 'locus of control'. Those students who scored high on the scale ('externals') believed that forces controlling their lives were external to themselves, in the hands of fate or chance. The students who were high 'externals' were more likely to drop out of high school than those who scored low on this attribute ('internals').

Parents are often surprised to learn how differently children and teenagers behave at school compared with what they know of their actions at home. As adolescents are taught, guided and disciplined by both parents and teachers, it would seem axiomatic that parent–teacher co-operation is beneficial. But many parents and teachers avoid co-operation. Parents may be afraid of 'interfering'; they may remember their own schooldays and their own sometimes forbidding teachers, and shy away from the opportunity to discuss things with them. So much depends on your approach.

A teenager with learning difficulties may be helped if you explore the range of possible causes and remedies with the teacher. You may know things he or she is not aware of and vice versa; putting your combined knowledge together could take you both to the root of the problem.

You may wish to broaden your contact with the school by attending 'open days' and parent–teacher associations. These contacts allow for informed exchanges. You can only gain if (without being intrusive) you stay in touch with what is happening to your offspring at school, as elsewhere.

Parents can help directly when their children have learning difficulties based upon poor skills at studying. There are four basic stages in the analysis of the skills required for effective study:

1 assessing the youngster's current level of skill (what is the problem?; how does one feel about it?; what can one actually do?);
2 setting a target or goal for study;
3 learning effectively;
4 reviewing the youngster's progress (monitoring).

At each of these stages, parents can offer their children quiet guidance about realistic targets for study; the planned use of study time (constructing a sensible timetable); advice about rewarding one's efforts with leisure time and/or treats; guided reading; attention to homework; quizzes and other 'fun' tests of progress made; plus other helpful ideas and moral support.

The flow chart (figure 5) provides a useful analysis of what may go wrong with homework tasks and may be indicative of more general learning problems.

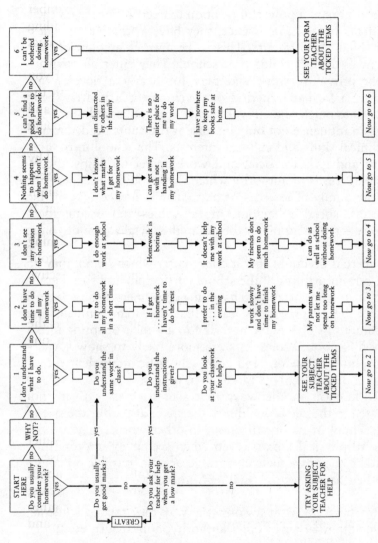

Figure 5   *Analysis of homework problems (Lancashire Health Authority (1979), Active Tutorial Work, book 2, Oxford: Blackwell)*

Rules and values at school

Schools are in a powerful position to exert influence on their students because, in essence, they have a 'captive audience' for some 15,000 hours. This is the average amount of time spent by British children at school. They enter an environment providing work and play for nearly a dozen years during a formative period of development. Children spend almost as much of their waking life at school as at home. And it is an influence not only because it transmits academic and technical skills and cultural interests. The school introduces boys and girls to social and working relationships and to various forms of authority which they would not experience in the family. The areas of particular influence – academic success, social behaviour, moral values and occupational choice – represent major themes in the socialization of young people.

There is no doubt that it does matter which school they go to; certain features of the school curriculum and social ethos are of vital importance to its young consumers. Many parents won't be surprised to learn that research confirms the assumptions they make in trying to get their offspring into a 'good' school. Adolescents *are* more likely to show socially acceptable behaviour and good scholastic attainment if they attend certain schools rather than others.

Differences in the ways that schools 'perform' are not related to the age of buildings, the space available, the size of the school or its organization. In other words, they are not due to physical factors, even when seemingly unpromising. Rather, they owe their favourable or unfavourable outcomes to their attributes as social *institutions*:

1 teacher actions in lessons (the way they talk to students, maintain an air of quiet authority, appear just, etc.);
2 the availability of incentives and rewards;
3 good conditions for pupils (a sense of being treated fairly, of having an interesting and useful curriculum, etc.);
4 opportunities for pupils to take on responsibility;

5 an emphasis on learning in a varied curriculum (an expectation that students are at school to learn, a pride in setting good standards, etc.).

The *cumulative* effect of various social factors is greater than the effect of any of the individual influences taken alone. The individual actions, approaches or measures combine to create a special ethos, or set of values, attitudes and behaviours which could be said to be characteristic of the school as a whole.

In a 1979 study of London secondary schools, Michael Rutter and a team of researchers found outcomes for pupils to be better when both the curriculum and approaches to discipline were agreed and supported by the staff acting together. Thus attendance was better and delinquency less frequent in schools where courses were planned jointly. Group planning provided opportunities for teachers to encourage and support one another. In addition, continuity of teaching was facilitated. Much the same was found with regard to standards of discipline. Examination successes were more frequent and delinquency less common in schools where discipline was based on general expectations set by the school (or department), rather than left to individual teachers to work out for themselves. School values and norms appear to be more effective if it is clear to all that they have widespread support.

Discipline is easier to maintain if the pupils appreciate that it relates to generally accepted approaches and does not simply represent the whims of the individual teacher. The particular rules which are set and the specific disciplinary techniques which are used are probably much less important than the establishment of some principles and guidelines which are clearly recognizable, and accepted by the school as a whole.

Truancy

Opting out is a way of life for the increasing number of pupils who truant. Truancy involves unlawful absence from school;

the word is derived from an Old French word meaning 'an assemblage of beggars'. In earlier centuries it had the connotation of 'a lazy, idle person, especially a boy who absents himself from school without leave ... one who wanders from an appointed place and neglects his duty or business' (*Oxford English Dictionary*). The association of truancy with vagrancy and villainy lingers on in modern thinking, since it is still referred to, in the light of its association with delinquency, as the kindergarten of crime.

Truancy should not be confused with school refusal, a psychological problem attributed either to anxieties about leaving home, particularly at times of family stress or illness, or to fears of school associated with bullying, fear of certain teachers and lessons, and so on (see chapter 3). Truancy is a very different phenomenon.

Some young people pretend to go to school and then slip away and spend the school hours elsewhere. Boys truant more frequently than girls. Truancy is a problem which increases steadily in incidence the older children get and is most frequent at age 13. However, a good deal of truancy goes on at the primary (elementary) school level. In general, a child's attendance record at school is a very good predictor of his or her adult adjustment. If non-attendance persists for long, it may result in educational backwardness with far-reaching effects upon emotional, social and occupational adjustment in later school life and in adulthood.

Underlying the truant's dislike for school is frequently a history of failure, often both academic and social. There have usually been several changes of school. Children who are poor at schoolwork (and truants tend to be in the lower range of academic achievement), and who are constantly criticized by their teachers and called stupid, find school a demoralizing experience. If they are kept down a year, they are likely to find school boring, lonely and embarrassing. They are stuck with younger children and are repeating work they have little feeling for and even less understanding of – a situation to escape from as soon as possible. Because over-age children generally fail to get social acceptance in the class, they make few friends, a factor which increases their rejection of school. Truancy is as powerful a deterrent to secondary school success as a low IQ. In any event, truants, on average, are below the majority of their schoolmates in mental ability and educational attainment. A few truants are of exceptional intelligence.

Persistent truants characteristically manifest problems such as enuresis, lying, stealing and aggression. Many offences such as shoplifting, stealing from cars, and so on, are committed by boys when they are roaming the streets during school hours.

Often, home conditions are intolerable for the truant, especially where marital disharmony causes rows and tension. In some cases homes are overcrowded and dirty, situated in slum areas, and parents may have little interest in their children's welfare; such families tend to be large, and their offspring may even lack adequate clothing. Some parents keep their children out of school apparently for no good reason. Many persistent truants have been rejected and thus lack affection or a close tie with a parent; many have slept out at night or run away from home. Children who truant tend to feel lonely and miserable, becoming unsociable and unable to persevere at anything.

Truants may have learned, over a period, that the best strategy for avoiding tensions at home – so often the source of harsh punishment and the scene of rows and rejection – is to escape. So they wander away from school (where they are often totally bored and anyway feel they are disliked by teachers and children alike) in the way they wander from home (where they also often feel unwanted). They may amuse themselves as solitaries; or may look for congenial companions who also crave excitement and a distraction from their feelings of depression and discouragement.

These are generalizations. There are many young people who truant – some occasionally, some frequently – who fit none of these patterns of home life or personality. Some truant because they have adopted their parents' don't-care attitude to education and authority, and the parents may tacitly consent to their children's truancy; such cases are difficult to deal with. Other children may truant just on rare occasions – for a dare, to escape an exam or a threatened punishment.

Fortunately firm parental pressure, reassurance about children's fears and understanding of their difficulties at school are sufficient to keep all but a small minority of rather seriously disturbed children regularly at school.

Persistent truancy may lead to a court appearance for the young person. In a recent British study of the effects of court procedures on truancy, 96 young people, of average age 13, appearing before the court for non-attendance at school, were randomly allocated to one of two court procedures. The adjourned group were repeatedly recalled to court to assess progress in school attendance; the interval between court appearances did not exceed six weeks. An interim care order was sometimes made if attendance at school was unsatisfactory, and if that proved ineffective a full care order was made. The supervised group were given supervision orders administered by either a social worker or a probation officer. It was found that, in the six months after the first court appearance for non-attendance at school, the children in the first group went back to school more frequently and committed fewer offences than those in the other group.

Parents may need to seek professional help for their truant children. Behavioural methods have been used successfully to deal with persistent truancy – programmes which often involve 'contingency' contracts. These are described in chapter 10.

Special educational units, small in scale and informal in style, have been set up in some British cities to deal with more intractable cases. Education welfare officers have (among other duties) the responsibility to investigate persistent non-attendance at school. Schools themselves have evolved different ways of coping with these (and other) problems. Some have instituted special pastoral care units. Similar experiments have been tried in the United States.

Disruptive pupils

In recent years there has been a mounting tide of public concern about violence and disruption in schools. Is the picture of mayhem in the classrooms a false image? One would like to think that this is yet another sensational, but baseless, portrayal of anarchy and chaos, lovingly nurtured by the media, in their search for good 'stories'. At times the public concern has a note of hysteria – what sociologists call moral panic. But what is disruptive behaviour? One might say that one pupil's eruption in class is another's disruption. Disruption involves interference with others so that they are prevented from doing something or are caused displeasure. This answer is deceptively simple. What teachers (or parents) define as disruptive depends upon their view of the essential nature of children in general, and pupils in particular. Teachers' perspectives range over a wide spectrum. At one extreme is the view of the 'good' student as deferential and docile – one who passively receives the wisdom and correct answers from the teachers. At the other extreme, the pupil is regarded as an *active* partner in the learning process – figuratively speaking the 'candle to be lit' rather than the 'vessel to be filled'. In this child-centred (as opposed to teacher-centred) approach, the child may be thought of as deviant if passive, whereas, in the other view, passivity is required of the good pupil. Not surprisingly what one teacher calls disruptive may not be so for another teacher.

Behaviour that is disruptive, in particular social and other interactions, occurs between:

1 pupil and authority (lateness, absenteeism, truancy, non-compliance);
2 pupil and work (repeated failure to do homework or produce written work, opposition to projected work);
3 pupil and teacher (the use of abusive and foul language, persistent interruption of the teacher, refusal to carry out instructions, disruptions of the teaching situation);
4 pupil and pupil (bullying, intimidation, violent assault, extortion, theft);

5 pupil and property (lack of care of books and equipment, defacing furniture, deliberate vandalism);
6 pupil and public (offences involving private property, public areas and public transport).

It helps to keep things in proportion when one remembers that nearly 10 million children in the United Kingdom attend school for 200 days in each school year. Certainly the number of serious *reported* incidents is not large in relation to all those pupil-hours.

In fact, we lack hard evidence about the incidence of disruptive or violent acts in schools. Nevertheless many teachers feel concerned and aggrieved and they describe disruptive pupils as unco-operative and rude, insolent and disobedient, provocative and aggressive, hostile and abusive, impertinent and argumentative, surly and arrogant, threatening and intimidating.

Evidence of 'concern' is not necessarily evidence that a problem exists in reality. But we cannot ignore the fact that many informed people feel there is indeed something seriously amiss in schools. My own experience, talking to and working with teachers and school administrators, suggests the existence of extreme indiscipline in a sizeable proportion of pupils in almost any class. The level of stress experienced by many teachers who are ill-prepared generally in classroom-management methods is worryingly high. Sadly, teachers are made to feel responsible for the outbursts of deviant behaviour by the more unruly pupils. As teachers (they are told and, indeed, feel) they should be able to control such provocations. But ultimately only the adolescent – usually a large and determined young adult – can control his or her own behaviour. Adolescents' behaviour is *their* responsibility.

Pupils who are described as 'disruptive' are far from being clones one of the other, as the label seems to imply. But they share, to a degree, certain attributes. They are inclined to truant, to have a low IQ and poor academic achievement. They tend to come from families which are inconsistent in their discipline, disharmonious in their relationships and in trouble over issues connected with finance and housing.

Aggressive children and teenagers tend to have suffered at the hands of parents who are extremely punitive, with attitudes that are cold, indifferent or rejecting. Supervision in the home is lax and erratic. Although not all children who are disruptive are emotionally disturbed, nevertheless many of them are. They manifest their disturbance by tending to interrupt, tease, talk and answer back at the wrong time, get out of their seats, pester, disobey and fight.

For many of these young people, academic lessons are incomprehensible and school is an irrelevancy. There is little that is fulfilling or reinforcing to be found inside the school. Low achievers, not surprisingly, hold negative attitudes towards school life; negative attitudes increase the risk of disruptive behaviour.

I ask the teachers at my 'workshops' on classroom management to think about what they would do if I were to address them throughout the day in (say) a language incomprehensible to them. (The analogy is not a perfect one, but many of the lessons must seem like a foreign language to grossly underachieving pupils who are conceptually impoverished, and, in some cases, almost illiterate.) The teachers usually describe a sequence of actions: restlessness, fidgeting, talking, distraction behaviour, complaining, hostility, walking out, staying away, and so on – in other words, classical disruptive behaviour.

Even the most aggressive pupils seem to 'choose' the teachers in whose classes they are particularly disruptive. In behaviour theory this is called 'situation specificity'. It is not enough simply to blame pupils as being 'disruptive' or 'obnoxious' in a global manner. Solutions are not produced by such generalities. It is more constructive to apply the problem-solving approach to the situation (see chapter 9). Why do they need to behave in this antisocial way? Can they not earn or receive sufficient esteem and other 'reinforcers' by socially acceptable actions? Do they get a 'pay-off' for their antisocial behaviour?

Pupils have very clear ideas about what offends their dignity, self-respect and self-esteem. They react against teachers who seem inhuman or too straitlaced, and who interpret their role as teachers too literally and rigidly; those who treat pupils as anonymous, or as members of a horde, rather than as individuals in their own right; teachers who are 'soft' and/or inconsistent; and those who are 'unfair'. By contrast, pupils describe a 'good teacher' as someone who is able to keep control (paradoxically, this attribute in particular); who is able to 'have a laugh' with you; who can generate warm, friendly relationships and who understands pupils; who is fair, treats them as equals or with respect; and who allows a degree of freedom.

The reactions to teachers who are felt (fairly or unfairly) to assail and affront pupils may involve strategies called 'equilibration' and 'reciprocation'. In the former, pupils use tactics to restore their sense of dignity and self-esteem; they most often take the form of truanting. The latter is a strategy which includes disruption; it is a form of 'paying back' in kind, insult for insult, blow for blow. The educationist Peter Woods (in a 1984 study) identified three major tactics of reciprocation:

1 'Subversive ironies' include the ridiculing of teachers by name-calling, writing insulting graffiti or playing tricks on them.
2 'Confrontational laughter' includes the sort of remark which raises the laughter of the entire class, at the teacher's expense.
3 'Symbolic rebellion' has been described in an example provided by Peter Woods. A class of fifth-year 'non-examination' boys were given the task of repairing and making functional two delapidated glasshouses. The job took them a whole term. They destroyed their work, when completed, in the space of a few minutes. This act seems like a comment on the pointlessness of school as far as they were concerned.

Teachers may be able to pre-empt or control such actions by looking out for vulnerable pupils – resentful young people who are predisposed to overreact to real or imagined insults.

Discipline and management in the classroom

There is a subtle but important distinction between managerial and educational outcomes of different disciplinary approaches. Both are important, and they overlap, but it is crucial to move beyond mere control. Since it cannot be assumed that quiet, orderly pupils are necessarily working in a productive or appropriate manner, discipline must arise not only from 'outer' control and from firm management but also from 'inner' control resulting from the pupil's interest and enthusiasm.

An educationist, J. W. Docking, in a 1985 paper, proposes two questions to teachers regarding their strategies for keeping order in the classroom:

1 As a result of these strategies, is the children's behaviour such that I can now go on to teach them something?
2 To what extent are these strategies making a direct contribution to the task of helping pupils to be successful in their learning and to develop an intrinsic interest in curriculum activities?

The style of discipline adopted by teachers has a marked effect on whether or not the pupil manifests acceptable behaviour. There is evidence that a humane approach to control, which is characterized by skilful *group* management, enhances pupil interest, motivation and achievement. It is particularly important for teachers to adopt strategies which convey purposefulness and seriousness, providing clear procedures for helping pupils and making pupils accountable for completing work on time.

The amount of formal punishment applied makes little difference in producing 'good behaviour'. In fact, too frequent disciplinary interventions are actually associated with increased disruptive activity in the classroom. Demeaning teaching behaviours such as corporal punishment, sarcasm or ridicule are notorious for militating against whatever educational outcomes are desired; in fact they tend to aggravate bad behaviour, and bring about alienation from school authority. There are parallels here with parental discipline.

Pointing out a pupil's good behaviour when it occurs, rather than focusing endlessly on the bad, and providing ample approval at appropriate times, will be of inestimable value to teachers who wish to foster benign attitudes and actions in their charges. Teachers, in general, find fault more than they praise.

If teachers pay attention to a pupil who is working well, this will tend to strengthen such activity and make it likely to recur. Building on this principle is what is called 'contingency management'. It embodies one of the main characteristics of behavioural approaches to classroom management; the systematic application to and/or withdrawal of reinforcement. The aim is to increase the desired academic-related actions and reduce the disruptive activities which are such a trial to everyone but the offender.

The most obvious and natural reinforcers available (and they are potent) are teachers' words of praise and encouragement, smiles, proximity, approval – in other words, their attention. For some under-achievers, the claim of that actress who said 'Rather bad publicity than *no* publicity at all!' seems to apply in the form: 'Rather negative attention (scolding) than no attention at all!' Teacher attention in the form of criticism and shouting can reinforce disruptive behaviour in certain children and thus, in making it more likely to recur, self-defeating. It is less likely to have this undesirable effect if it takes the form of a 'soft reprimand'; a quiet, perhaps whispered caution, does not place the pupil in the limelight of attention from classmates.

Psychologists have applied principles of operant conditioning (see chapter 10) to supplant inattentive (and disruptive) behaviour by strengthening socially and academically acceptable activities that are incompatible with the undesirable 'off task' behaviours such as squirming, fooling, talking, tapping and walking around the classroom.

Differential reinforcement is used to strengthen attending ('on task') actions, such as looking at the book, working out the maths problem, or listening to – and communicating with

– the teacher, at appropriate times. Appropriate behaviour is rewarded (with praise, privileges, etc.), while inappropriate actions are ignored (if possible) or penalized.

There is a caveat to all of this. Teachers are often advised without qualification to reward pupils for their good behaviour rather than punish them for their bad behaviour. Rewards handed out indiscriminately carry the risk of undermining intrinsic motivation – the inherent interest and reward of the task itself. As Samuel Johnson observed, 'He who praises everybody praises nobody.'

There can be a joy in learning and mastering a skill. Verbal praise, as distinct from tangible rewards, tends to enhance rather than reduce intrinsic interest. This is because verbal praise can provide youngsters with information ('feedback') about their performance. The language of praise is crucial. The words 'Great! I like the way you are using trial and error to solve that problem' are more fruitful, in their specificity, than monosyllabic approbation such as 'Great!', 'Good', or the more verbose 'Well done!' Rewards are more likely to increase youngsters' curiosity, desire to respond to a challenge and satisfaction with their work if they are sincere, justified and made contingent on quality of achievement.

Psychologists have been able (by systematically varying teachers' attention) to change an initially well-behaved class with an average rate of disruptiveness of 8.7 per cent to one in which disruptiveness reached a level, on average, of 25.5 per cent. This increase was made possible by getting the teachers to withhold approval when pupils were being attentive. When the old conditions were restored, disruptiveness decreased to 12.0 per cent. It rose to 19.4 per cent on return to these non-approval conditions, and then soared to 31 per cent when teachers strongly and frequently disapproved of disruptive behaviour. Fortunately, normality was finally reinstated when the experiment was terminated. These are not ephemeral or frivolous results. They have been replicated many times and they enshrine an important principle.

This emphasis on the 'positive' is not a recipe for letting

children 'get away with' deviant behaviour. Judicious ignoring can work for certain subliminal or barely perceptible infractions which are designed to attract attention. More serious transgressions would lead to chaos if they were simply ignored, and if nothing else was done. Teachers who are most effective at managing their classes tend to spot disruptive actions very early on an then nip them in the bud with minimum fuss and drama but nevertheless firmly. The net effect is negligible interruption of the class and minimum 'pay-offs' for offenders from their classmates.

Among various factors to be borne in mind when planning management strategies, there is a common theme which applies to disruption at home as well as at school. The fraught atmosphere which arises from *frequent* disciplinary interventions – the tensions and resentments that are generated – may contribute to a widening and intensification of the disruption. Constant criticism, nagging and reprimands (a negative home or school atmosphere of unremitting disapproval) increase the likelihood that youngsters will show hostile behaviour.

Physical punishment (caning, smacking) tends to aggravate tense situations and has been shown to provoke social aggression in the punished. It is too easy to apply (it doesn't take much thought), and its results are difficult to justify.

Another factor to be considered is that high expectations of children – whether in academic performance or behaviour – tend to produce high-level behaviour; and low expectations tend to be 'confirmed' by low-level performance. This is the notorious 'self-fulfilling prophecy'.

Giving children responsibility for looking after school books and equipment conveys teachers' expectations that they will behave responsibly; young people can similarly be taught to behave responsibly at home. It should always be remembered that they are responsible for their own behaviour – good and bad. In the final analysis the teacher cannot control, or be responsible for, a young adult's actions. If the teacher's attitude implies that adolescents are not ultimately in control of their own behaviour, they will be tempted to opt out of their responsibilities. It is important to achieve a subtle balance between your authority and the teenager's self-direction and accountability.

It is also essential for young people to understand precisely what kind of behaviour is regarded as disruptive. Just as parents are wise to condemn the act ('I don't like what you are doing') rather than the teenager ('I don't like you any more because you . . .'), teachers who rebuke the action ('I think that action was . . .') rather than the youngster ('I think you are, as always, contemptible') will make it easier for the pupil to define the deviant behaviour as atypical and to avoid the temptation to do it in the future.

In the light of these considerations, I offer the following guidelines for good practice in the classroom. They apply equally to parents.

1 Keep the would-be disrupter out of the limelight; make sure you remain centre stage.
2 Try to spot the trouble as it begins; nip it in the bud.
3 Keep your interventions to a minimum; when you intervene, be firm, authoritative and (if at all possible, even if you have to pretend) cool.
4 Avoid physical punishment.
5 Find a realistic level of aspiration for the youngster, not impossibly high, nor patronizingly low.
6 Teach adolescents to be responsible by giving them responsibility and by letting them accept their responsibilities.
7 Focus on *acts* rather than 'personalities'.
8 Foster, warm, caring relationships.
9 Try to enhance or improve the youngster's self-image.
10 Set fair but firm and consistent limits.
11 Plan a varied and stimulating educational programme.

Although these approaches are useful, they could be difficult to put into practice for the more seriously disruptive adolescents, in the existing structure of many of our large present-day schools. Some schools have created schools-within-schools in order to deal with children with special needs; some educational authorities have set up special educational units for those youngsters who do not 'fit in'. The success of such provision – such as it is – is attributed to:

increased opportunities for pupils to exercise responsibility;
informal pupil–teacher relationships;
provision for independent study;
opportunities for off-campus study;
procedures for sharing in democratic decision-making;
flexible sharing;
making the curriculum relevant;
reducing class sizes;
providing tutorials;
providing courses;
shortening school days;
bringing in people from outside to teach.

More specifically, the teacher can adopt (in such settings) a tactical approach to the management of disruptive pupils by means of behavioural and other individualized methods (see chapter 10).

Chapter Nine

Ways of helping young people

When I was fourteen my father was so stupid I could hardly stand to have him around. At twenty-one I was astonished at how much he had learned in the past seven years.

(Mark Twain)

Many young people come to the realization belatedly that their parents are much wiser than they gave them credit for. It is important to remember, if you ever doubted it, that adults – parents, teachers, friends and relatives – can be of immense help to teenagers. There *are* times to remain silent, but there are times when silence and inactivity on the part of parents come very close to Francis Bacon's admonition that 'silence is the virtue of fools'. Teenagers who experience problems *can* be helped by sharing your knowledge and hard-won experience. Adolescents may not be easy to help; indeed, there may be an initial reaction of prickly disdain. But when they face really tough decisions most *are* open to sensitively and sensibly proffered guidance. People are most susceptible to influence during periods of rapid change, and we have seen how adolescence is a period of flux.

One of the difficulties of counselling certain adolescents is their overreaction to a previously childish and over-idealized view of parental omnipotence. Here is a young student, in late adolescence, commenting on this phenomenon:

Until I was a teenager I thought my father was perfect. That is not to say I didn't have disagreements with him, but they were disagreements with an important stipulation: he was always right. It wasn't that he beat me or something until I admitted to him that he was right – he rarely physically punished me, I just always felt that although we might have a difference of opinion, it was ordained that he was in the right, or, rather, that I was in the wrong.

I guess the reason I thought my father was perfect for such a long time is that whenever we do anything together, he always gives advice and I always follow it, so it took me a long time to discover that there is more than one correct way to do everything. When I don't follow his advice, it leaves me feeling anxious, like I've done something wrong in opposing him. I also notice an interesting occurrence when we have disagreements: I stop thinking. As soon as he says, 'Why did you . . . ?' or 'Why don't you . . . ?' my mind simply shuts down.

As we all experience the upheaval of radical changes in our circumstances at one time or another, we should (in theory) be sympathetic to what is happening to our offspring. But sympathy is not always enough. Parents wish to be of help in practical ways. Even something as apparently simple as giving advice may not be quite as straightforward as it sounds.

There are several ways in which you (or a professional) can help or support an adolescent through a difficult patch. Sometimes you may be able to do something directly on your child's behalf – for example, acting as a mediator in a quarrel or putting a stop to bullying. Sometimes you may be able to change the external circumstances (perhaps by improving other people's attitudes or the aggravating circumstances) which are the cause of your teenager's difficulties. If you cannot change the circumstances, you may have to rely on modifying the adolescent's perception of or reaction to them. Other methods are described in the following pages. These approaches are *not* mutually exclusive; they overlap in practice and, indeed, converge in the 'behavioural approach', discussed at the end of the chapter.

Teaching life skills

There are a thousand and one social graces and nuances which make social life easy and pleasurable for all concerned (see figure 6). They require skills – such as confidence, sensitivity and the ability to form accurate impressions of

ME AND YOU	ME	ME AND SPECIFIC SITUATIONS
Skills I need to relate effectively to you	Skills I need to manage and grow	Skills I need for my education
○ how to communicate effectively ○ how to make, keep and end a relationship ○ how to give and get help ○ how to manage conflict ○ how to give and receive feedback	○ how to read and write ○ how to achieve basic numeracy ○ how to find information and resources ○ how to think and solve problems constructively ○ how to identify my creative potential and develop it ○ how to manage time effectively ○ how to make the most of the present ○ how to discover my interests ○ how to discover my values and beliefs ○ how to set and achieve goals ○ how to take stock of my life ○ how to discover what makes me do the things I do ○ how to be positive about myself ○ how to cope with and gain from life transitions ○ how to make effective decisions ○ how to be proactive (make things happen) ○ how to manage negative emotions ○ how to cope with stress ○ how to achieve and maintain physical wellbeing ○ how to manage my sexuality	○ how to discover the education options open to me ○ how to choose a course ○ how to study
		Skills I need at work
		○ how to discover the job options open to me ○ how to find a job ○ how to keep a job ○ how to change jobs ○ how to cope with unemployment ○ how to achieve a balance between my job and the rest of my life ○ how to retire and enjoy it
		Skills I need at home
		○ how to choose a style of living ○ how to maintain a home ○ how to live with other people
		Skills I need for leisure
		○ how to choose between leisure options ○ how to maximize my leisure opportunities ○ how to use my leisure to increase my income
ME AND OTHERS		
Skills I need to relate effectively to others		Skills I need in the community
○ how to be assertive ○ how to influence people and systems ○ how to work in groups ○ how to express feelings constructively ○ how to build strength in others		○ how to be a skilled consumer ○ how to develop and use my political awareness ○ how to use public facilities

Figure 6   Life skills (copyright © Barrie Hopson and Mike Scally, Lifeskills Associates, Leeds)

others – which many adults take for granted, having acquired them apparently without too much thought or difficulty. However, there are many people, both children and adults, who lack some of the crucial skills required to cope with life in a constructive and adaptive manner.

If children can be helped to become more competent at social skills, then they may have less recourse to maladaptive behaviour. These skills include improving powers of observation and accurate judgement; basic conversation skills such as listening, asking questions and talking; expressive skills such as the use of body language; social techniques for special situations; self-assertion training, and so on. These and other skills break down essentially into the three groups shown in table 4.

Table 4   *Three types of social skills*

Observational skills	Performance skills	Cognitive skills
Getting information	Verbal skills	Planning
Reading social signals	Non-verbal expression	Problem-solving
Asking questions	Greetings and partings	
	Rewarding skills	
	Assertive skills	

The psychologists Michael Argyle and Peter Trower draw an analogy in their book *Person to Person: Ways of Communicating* between social behaviour and driving a car. This is not as far-fetched as it sounds. Both have goals: a car driver sets out to go somewhere, and so, in effect, does someone in a social interaction. Both are skilled performances, at which some individuals are 'naturals' and others, sadly, very poor.

In training someone in social skills – say, conversational skills – you would rehearse with him or her the different types of conversational 'journey', each with its own goal. One type is simply to communicate information; another might be to get to know someone and to enjoy a social relationship. The authors make the point that steering a conversation is like navigating a car, so you would rehearse with the youngster the signs and signals (the 'feedback') given by the other person(s). If one cannot recognize these signs, one is likely to be as lost as the person who cannot read a road map.

A motorist has to make complex, quick and synchronized adjustments to road conditions, and these are performed unconsciously and smoothly by the skilled driver. Feedback in a conversation comes from looking at the other person's facial expression, and also from what he or she says, as well as a lot of non-verbal sounds like 'uh-huh', behaviours like head-nods, or disapproving frowns, together with phrases like 'I see' or 'really'. In their totality these messages (not everyone interprets them accurately or even notices them) tell us whether we are on 'dangerous territory' – pursuing, say, a painful topic or a subject of great sensitivity to the other person – or on safe ground. Adjustments have to be made in the tone and direction of conversations if they are to be amiable and likely to make the other person wish to talk to you again. There are many rules in social interaction just as there are rules of the road. They have to be understood.

Even young people with poor social skills are likely to have several effective *components* of socially skilled behaviours, for example a warm smile and good eye contact. These can be built on, improved and polished by instruction, or by feedback and prompts, during role rehearsal. Role rehearsal allows you to comment on the youngster's performance. It is a gradual process – building up the various components making up a particular skill. This sort of rehearsal provides an intermediate step in changing behaviour and developing new and more effective strategies. The endpoint is when the teenager tries out the new skill or role in real life.

To take one application: self-effacing, timid youngsters may overcome these difficulties by training in assertion. They practise asserting themselves in an imaginary situation, such as a confrontation with a shopkeeper who has given the wrong change, or asking a member of the opposite sex to a party. The difficulty of the situations is gradually increased. The youngsters then assert themselves in relatively easy real-life settings, before tackling more challenging circumstances.

Role rehearsal involves the following steps:

1 Demonstrate the skill.
2 Ask the young person to practise the skill. (Use role play. Provide a model if necessary.)
3 Provide feedback about the accuracy/inaccuracy of the performance. (It is particularly advantageous for the youngster to evaluate the effectiveness of his or her own performance, and video equipment is most useful here.)
4 Give practice assignments, e.g. real-life planned practice or the try-out of skills at home. Not only does this provide for acquiring new skills but it also allows their practice at a controlled pace and in a safe environment, and in this way minimizes distress.

The psychologists Arthur Lange and Patricia Jakubowski, authors of *Responsible Assertive Behaviour*, suggest the sort of feedback to give young people practising their role in a situation fraught with the potential for hostile conflict or humiliating retreat. It could be a student asking a teacher not to make racist jokes.

1 Start off with the strengths of the performance. Specify exactly which behaviours were positive.

Verbal behaviours
Was the statement direct and to the point?
Was the statement firm but not hostile?
Did the statement show some consideration, respect, or recognition of the other person?
Did the statement accurately reflect the speaker's goals?
Did the statement leave room for escalation?
If the statement included an explanation, was it short rather than a series of excuses?
Did the statement include sarcasm, pleading, or whining?

Did the statement blame the other person for the speaker's feelings?

Nonverbal behaviours
Was eye contact present?
Was the speaker's voice level appropriately loud?
Was the statement filled with pauses?
Did the speaker look confident or were nervous gestures or inappropriate laughter present?
Was the statement flat or expressive?

2 After all positive feedback has been given, offer feedback suggestions.

Describe the behaviour, rather than give a label. Be objective rather than judgemental.

Offer a possible way of improvement. This should be expressed in a tentative rather than absolute manner. Do not impose a suggestion.

Ask the group member for a reaction to the suggestions, allowing the member to accept, refuse, or modify the suggestion.

There seem to be two basic conditions which should be enhanced if friendships and other social relations are going to come with reasonable ease. The social skills trainer will wish to know whether the teenager (a) perceives other people primarily as sources of satisfaction rather than deprivation; (b) has opportunities for social interactions that reward and make enjoyable the giving, as well as the receiving, of affection? If not, he or she needs to ask the questions 'Why not?' and 'Is there anything I can do to change those negative conditions?'

Role play

Psychologists have helped teenagers (and their parents) to resolve conflicts by the use of role play. The adolescent is encouraged to perform a normal role which is not usually his or her own, or asked to perform a normal role but not in a setting where it is usually enacted. The method is used to teach young people very basic skills, to help them become more effective in their interactions, and to help them to become more confident when extremely anxious (e.g. through enacting scences such as talking to the police, going to an interview with an employer or dealing with provocation).

It can be illuminating to ask the child and the adult (parent) to reverse or change roles, the youngster playing parent or vice versa. One or other can pretend to be the individual who is thought to be the source of the problem. This technique can lead to new insights and even the development of empathy.

There is a method of helping young people to test out the way they perceive (and self-defeatingly misconstrue) their world. It is useful for youngsters (and, indeed, their parents) who have low self-esteem, feel persecuted and are lacking in confidence.

1 The person is encouraged to explore (by trying out) patterns of behaviour contrasted to his or her own. This is based on a carefully scripted role – a sketch worked out with the youngster and derived from a compromise between what he or she is 'actually' like, and what he or she would like to be like.
2 The adolescent is invited to practise these patterns in everyday life.
3 From practice the person gains an experience of how the environment can differ in appearance and 'feel', and how it reacts, when *he* or *she* behaves in a different manner.
4 Practice generates new and more effective skills, supplemented by novel experience from the feedback received.
5 The expectation is that by receiving new and helpful forms of feedback from the environment the adolescent will change the self-defeating attitudes that control his or her behaviour.

Here is an example of role play by a parent, provided in her own words by the mother of one of my child patients:

We discussed childrearing and why I had become so tentative in dealing with Tommy. We also discussed my parents' way of bringing me up and how it had influenced my attitudes. The hardest problem to deal with was the self-doubt and isolation. Being depressed for several years and feeling inadequate, a failure, had eroded my self-confidence and produced a profound dislike for myself. It was necessary to change that before I could look up and outwards.

Dr H. asked me to role-play as a means of learning new ways of coping with my fears and suspicions of people. I started by writing a self-portrait. (Rereading it recently, I was struck by its negative qualities.) Dr H. took each point and changed it to some extent. Where I was serious, introverted, careful, I was to be rather more spontaneous and impulsive, even a little frivolous – without 'overdoing' it. I was to think and act like an attractive woman; in fact we created a different persona and role from my usual ones, but not too far removed (he said) from reality to make the task impossible. We went over it in great detail like a script.

The next step was not easy. What I had to do was go out and live my role daily. Privately I thought Dr H. was probably insane! It was certainly very difficult at first. You feel like a second-rate actor with severe stage-fright. But the remarkable thing was how it gradually became easier; and when the results were good I felt elated. I discovered casual conversations with local mothers, in the park or at the shops, soon unearthed common interests, and I gradually developed new friendships with women in similar circumstances to myself, all with children for Tommy and Claire to play with. For the first time since Tommy's birth we were making regular visits outside the immediate family. Social skills are like any other. The more practice you get, the better you become. As my confidence grew with each success, so Tommy also relaxed, and he began to look forward to these visits eagerly.

Throughout this period, during which there were regularly held discussions about my own situation and problems, we also worked on Tommy's problems.

Devised by the eminent American personality theorist and clinician, George Kelly, fixed-role therapy is a sophisticated form of behaviour rehearsal, or what is more generally referred to as behavioural-cognitive work.

Cognitive learning and control (problem-solving)

Behaviour is not always predictable from external sources of influence; cognitive factors (thinking processes) in part determine what we observe, feel and do at any particular point in time. Cognitive learning is a generic term for learning about the world by the use of reasoning, judgement, imagination, and various perceptual and conceptual abilities. Such learning makes use of images, symbols, concepts and rules. There are signs of a growing interest in training children and adolescents in problem-solving and in cognitive control. Whereas the nature of the cognitive problems associated with adult anxiety and depression – to take two examples – can be conceptualized as *cognitive errors*, the cognitive problems and the focus of treatment in cognitive-behavioural therapy with children or immature adolescents are most often *cognitive absences*. The child fails to engage in the cognitive, information-processing activities of an active problem-solver and refrains from initiating the reflective thought processes that can control behaviour. Indeed he or she may lack the cognitive skills needed to carry out crucial abstract, analytical mental activities.

Much of what we think of as 'emotional disturbance' can be viewed in an alternative way: as the consequence of ineffective behaviour and thinking. The individual is unable to resolve certain dilemmas in his or her life: the unproductive attempts to do so have adverse effects such as anxiety, conflict and depression, not to mention the creation of additional problems. For parents (or teachers) the way to decode teenagers' sometimes incomprehensible actions is to ask oneself what they are trying to achieve – seen from their point of view. Their 'solutions' may produce immediate benefits which, for that reason, are difficult to discard, even though they involve unacceptable or self-defeating actions. Does the 'tunnel vision' of their inexperience and immaturity stop them from seeing how unprofitable their chosen course of action is, over the longer term? Does their lack of particular skills deny to them alternative courses of action which would be more socially acceptable?

Problematic behaviours in adolescence, according to this way of thinking, arise as a consequence of the young person's failure to learn successful ways of coping with his or her environment or as the result of applying inappropriate stategies to the challenges of life. How, then, does one overcome such an impasse?

You can help your teenager (and, indeed, yourself) when under pressure, by adopting the problem-solving approach. In this method 'small' is not so much 'beautiful' as 'manageable'. Problems are not manageable when they are conceived in large global terms ('*Everything* is going wrong'; 'He will *never* change'; 'There is *no* hope'; 'I seem to have the world on my shoulders.' No one can cope with problems when they are pitched at this cosmological level, a tendency called 'catastrophizing'. But apparently 'enormous' problems can be reduced to their proper size by an 'unravelling' process which gets to the nub of things, discarding the irrelevant or less important elements. The process of identifying the *core* of the problem (and whose it is) requires you to examine all sides of the question, establishing and obtaining the relevant facts. This exercise has a calming effect when panic or misery is clouding everyone's judgement. It is also reassuring.

If an adolescent says 'there is no future' and that 'life is awful; no one likes me', you can begin by drawing up a *balance sheet* with its credit and debit columns. Tease out with your child the pluses in his or her life, the good points in terms of personality, talents, physical characteristics and verbal skills. Now look at their perception of the negatives (which may not always be as negative as they judge). Divide up the list into items that are irremediable ('I'm not tall enough'; 'My breasts are too large') and those that are remediable ('I'm fat'; 'I don't know how to make small talk to boys/girls'; 'I always feel shy'). You can help your youngster to be philosophical about shortness or 'bosominess', and to put the proper emphasis, which should be very little, on such matters. Diet, properly supervised, will bring about a better body-image and thus self-image. And attention to social skills will enhance his or her low self-esteem which is the nub of the problem. As long as they see the problem in 'cosmological' terms of there being no future, of life being awful, there is not much to be done. Once the problem is unpacked, one can see several possibilities for positive action.

To the extent that you can adopt a *mental attitude* of believing that you *can* cope with a problem, the greater is the likelihood that you will come up with a solution to it. The feeling of being in control (and, therefore, *not* helpless) is vital to the successful working through of difficult situations. You 'relabel' the problem you once thought of as impenetrable as 'manageable', given thought and calm application of the problem-solving approach.

Although it is a cliché, the saying 'Think first, act afterwards' is none the less worth remembering. To act impulsively is often to think regretfully afterwards of the disastrous outcome, of what *might* have been done differently, and more rationally. The strategy is to attempt to control events rather than letting them control us.

Problem-solving skills provide us with a general coping strategy for a variety of difficult situations. They could help teenagers taught by psychologists (in more serious circumstances) or by parents to deal more effectively with a variety of conflict situations, such as choosing between alternative courses of action, arriving at mutually acceptable decisions with parents, developing co-operation with the peer group. The particular advantage of the problem-solving approach is that it teaches people how to think and work things out for themselves. There are four steps:

1 *General orientation*. This is by way of an introductory scene-setting exercise; trying with the young person's help to gain some perspective about the nature of the problem, putting it into context of why, when and how it occurs. It is important that he or she should be able to recognize the problem and the 'danger' signs. The youngster might think back over the events that have given rise in the past to the problem situation. If this sheds no light on the difficulty you might encourage your daughter or son to monitor future circumstances that prove problematic (e.g. a diary of events).

2 *Problem definition and formulation*. Define all aspects of the problem as explicitly as possible, in concrete terms rather than in vague and abstract language. This helps you to unravel what looks like a complicated problem and, perhaps to simplify it. Here is an example (an agoraphobic adolescent): 'It is a terrible effort to shop at the centre. I begin to get butterflies in my stomach when I go into the shopping centre. I feel nervous if there is a large crowd milling about. I can just about cope with small shops if I stay near the door. I really begin to panic if I have to shop in the large shops, well in or away from the door. Before long I feel paralysed, I can't move; I feel as if I might faint.' And here is an example for parents: 'I get angry with my son David. My muscles tense up. I want to lash out at him when he is cheeky. But what do I mean when I say he's cheeky? It's when I feel that my dignity is threatened, especially when my friends are present, or that my authority is demeaned. It's something about his manner, dumb insolence I call it, unfriendly. And then, eventually, I explode in a torrent of recrimination and abuse. Perhaps he also feels provoked by my manner. I must think about that.'

Next you might categorize the salient features of the particular situation in a way that identifies your main *goals* and the *obstacles* that get in the way of fulfilling these goals. For example, the agoraphobic teenager wishes to be able to shop normally, i.e. without anticipatory dread (her goal). To do that she will have to overcome her anxiety (the barrier). David's mother wishes to improve her relationship with her son (the goal), her interpretation of his motives and manner and possibly her own attitude towards him (if he says she is patronizing, this may be a barrier to her objective). This stage is a further clarification of what may be going wrong and why this should be so.

3 *Setting goals.* Setting goals is at the centre of the attempt to solve problems; your help in this matter could be invaluable to your teenager. A *workable* goal is an accomplishment that helps the individual manage problematic situations. The goal is achieved when he or she has acquired new skills, practised them, and actually used them to solve or manage the situation causing all the difficulties. This accomplishment is often referred to in counselling as the new (or preferred) scenario.

Here are some scenarios based on questions adolescents can usefully ask themselves:

Q   What would the problem situation be like if I could cope better?
A   I'd be able to talk to others without feeling awkward and tongue-tied; I would not spend so much time on my own.

Q   What changes would take place in my lifestyle?
A   I'd go out with a nice girl. I'd be more ambitious; take an interest.

Q   What would be happening that is not happening now?
A   I'd go to concerts, the cinema and plays instead of always moping in front of the TV.

Scenarios and set goals can help teenagers in difficulty, in four ways:

(a) They focus the person's attention and action. They provide a vision which offers hope and an outlet for concentrated effort.
(b) They mobilize energy and help pull the worrier out of the inertia of helplessness and depression.

(c) They enhance the persistence needed for working at the problem.

(d) They motivate people to search for strategies to accomplish their goals.

If you can help adolescents to the point of defining goals, they are, in essence, on the first stage of 'recovery' – orientating themselves to face life rather than turning away from it, embracing optimism rather than resignation. Gerard Egan, a distinguished theorist and practitioner in the field of counselling, writes (1986) that goals should preferably be:

(a) *specific*, a necessity if they are to be converted into actions;

(b) *measurable*, that is, capable of providing feedback that change is occurring and, eventually, verifying that the objective has been accomplished;

(c) *realistic*, in the sense that the adolescent has the resources to achieve them; that external circumstances are not bound to thwart their accomplishment; that the goals are under the control (potentially) of the teenager; and the cost of obtaining them is not too high;

(d) *pertinent to their problem* and not simply a partial solution or even a diversionary move;

(e) *the adolescent's own goals* and not those he or she simply adopts because someone expects them of him/her, or they are the line of least resistance;

(f) *in keeping with his or her values*;

(g) *achievable within a reasonable time*.

The problem-solving approach is geared to the present and the future rather than being preoccupied with past wrongs, mistakes and 'complexes'. Thus a young man of 19 (Graham) who saw his friend – a pillion passenger on his motor bike – badly injured while he was unharmed is tortured by remorse. He drinks heavily and obsessively asks himself whether the accident was his fault. His studies at university have suffered and his social life has dwindled to nothing. He spends all his free time at the hospital where his friend is making a slow and painful recovery, but one which will never allow him to be the promising athlete he was. The friends avoid talking about the accident.

Graham is helped to spell out a scenario in which he makes his peace with his friend by raising the painful subject of the accident, and by expressing his sorrow (and sense of responsibility) for what happened. He will visit his friend regularly but not 'hound' his bedside in the guilt-ridden, self-punishing way that has been his previous practice. He will begin to pick up the threads with his other friends, and apply himself to his studies as a counter to the obsessive thoughts he has when sitting around indulging in morbid introspection.

4 *Action*. In taking action to deal with a problem there are three substages which help you or your youngster to make the right move and to verify that you have done so.

(i) *Generation of alternatives*. Work out as wide a range of possible solutions as you can think of in terms of general strategies (what to do) and, later, specific tactics to implement the general strategy (how to do it). Brainstorming – freely and, at first, uncritically generating as many ideas as possible – can be a help. For example: the phobic girl can continue to try to solve her problem on her own, but she has done this to no avail. She can consult a clinical psychologist. Let us look at the way David's mother puts the alternatives:

(a) I could punish David more severely.
(b) I could ignore him.
(c) I could try to engage in a calm debate with him.
(d) I could turn the issue over to his father.
(e) I could penalize him (take away a proportion of his pocket money each time) without getting into an interminable debate.
(f) I could negotiate an agreement with him covering the perennial issues we argue over.
(g) I could look into my own attitudes and feelings toward him. Do *I* get *him* going as much as he does me? Am I at fault in some way?

It might be useful to ask others how they would react, or imagine how others might react, if requested to solve a similar problem (e.g. how would his father, aunt or his teacher approach this problem?).

(ii) *Decision-making*. Work out the likely consequences of the better courses of action you have put forward. What is the utility of these consequences in resolving the problem as it has been formulated? For exampie, with regard to the proposed solutions:

(a) Punishment doesn't seem to work; in fact it seems to make David more intractable.
(b) He'd probably follow me around, arguing more forcibly. Like me, he can be very stubborn.
(c) Sounds good, but I find it so hard to keep cool. And we may not be able to resolve things in the heat of the particular confrontation.
(d) My husband won't thank me for that; he'll say, 'It's your problem.' I have to cope in *my* way when David is disobedient.
(e) This may work but it could also generate trouble, sulking and tantrums.
(f) Sounds a possibility; David can be reasonable when he's in a good mood. The trick is to catch him at the right time.
(g) This is painful, but he may have a point when he says he wishes I could hear myself talk to him as if he's an idiot or baby.

(iii) *Choosing between alternative strategies*. Any decision to change is likely to involve benefits and 'costs': benefits for oneself (it is hoped), for significant others, for one's social network. There could be costs to oneself, to others and to one's social setting. Gerard Egan suggests a balance sheet to help the person work through the implications of his or her chosen course of action (see figure 7).

(iv) *Verification*. Try out the most acceptable and feasible-looking solution. Monitor your chosen course of action and

If I choose this course of action:		
The self		
Gains for self:	Acceptable to me because:	Not acceptable to me because:
Losses for self:	Acceptable to me because:	Not acceptable to me because:
Significant others		
Gains for significant others:	Acceptable to me because:	Not acceptable to me because:
Losses for significant others:	Acceptable to me because:	Not acceptable to me because:
Social setting		
Gains for social setting:	Acceptable to me because:	Not acceptable to me because:
Losses for social setting:	Acceptable to me because:	Not acceptable to me because:

Figure 7   Balance sheet of results of a chosen course of action
(G. Egan (1986) The Skilled Helper, *Monterey: Brooks/Cole)*

its consequences. Try to match the actual outcomes against the hoped-for outcomes; if the match is satisfactory, you 'exit' (to use the jargon) much relieved; if not, you continue to 'operate', which means that you return to the beginning of the sequence of problem-solving operations and start again.

Reconsider the original problem in the light of this attempt of yours at problem-solving. Do not be put off if you fail; try again. 'Experience' is based upon trial and error, and learning from one's mistakes. Work out new solutions.

The phobic youngster could well be provided by the psychologist with a refinement of the problem-solving approach; a series of self-statements (a sort of script) in order to cope with her fear. D. H. Meichenbaum (in a 1974 study) has offered the following example:

Preparing for a stressful event:
> What is it you have to do?
> You can develop a plan to deal with it.
> Just think about what you can do about it.
> That's better than getting anxious.
> No negative self-statements; just think rationally.
> Don't worry: worry won't help anything.
> Maybe what you think is anxiety is eagerness to confront the situation.

Confronting and handling a stressful event:
> Just psych yourself up – you can meet this challenge.
> You can convince yourself to do it. You can reason your fear away.
> One step at a time; you can handle the situation.
> Don't think about fear; just think about what you have do do. Stay relevant.
> This anxiety is what the doctor said you would feel.
> It's a reminder to use your coping exercises.
> Relax, you're in control. Take a slow deep breath.

Coping with the feeling of being overwhelmed:
> When fear comes, just pause.

Keep the focus on the present; what is it you have to do?

Label your fear from 0 to 10 and watch it change. You should expect your fear to rise.

Don't try to eliminate fear totally; just keep it manageable.

Reinforcing self-statements:

It worked; you did it.

Wait until you tell your therapist (or group) about this.

It wasn't as bad as you expected.

Your damn ideas – that's the problem. When you control them, you control your fear.

It's getting better each time you use the procedures.

You can be pleased with the progress you're making.

You did it!

Teenagers, not uncommonly, find themselves coping with explosive feelings of frustration which lead to anger and (when not controlled) to verbal abuse or physical aggression. A clinical psychologist, R. W. Novaco, has developed techniques for reducing the global sense of anger to its constituent elements to bring it under control. (An example of his method is given in chapter 10.)

Professional counselling

If your teenager's problems prove intractable, you may want to consider calling on the assistance of a professional counsellor. Counselling has as its main aim the production of constructive behavioural and personality change. Such change requires a relationship of trust, one which emerges from confidential conversations between the professionally trained person and the adolescent.

It is not easy to specify the point at which the alarm bells ring so that you call in outside help. People tend to seek assistance when the problems persist in being 'bizarre' or not understandable, when they are unpredictable and when they resist control. One tends to think of behaviour or emotions as problematic when they become frequent in their manifestation and/or reach a high level of intensity.

The eminent theorist on counselling, Carl Rogers, describes the process as a freeing of the 'growth capacities' of the individual, which permits him or her to acquire 'more mature' ways of acting and reacting which are less fraught with anxiety or conflict. He is talking about a learning process within a humanistic, rather than behaviourist, context.

The attributes of the counsellor which are known to facilitate such learning are ones which some parents do (or should) adopt naturally, in counselling their own off-spring:

1 *genuineness and authenticity:* the conveying of 'realness' to clients (children) through the counsellor 'being himself';
2 *non-possessive warmth:* the attitude of friendly concern and caring;
3 *accurate empathy:* the capacity to see things from the clients' (child's) point of view, to 'feel with' them, so that they feel they are understood.

The psychoanalyst Martha Harris (in her 1969 book) says, for the benefit of parents, that 'we can try to feel ourselves back into that contradiction of arrogance and abasement which the teenager experiences and presents himself as being. By our re-experience of the contradiction in our imagination we are able to adjust the tone of our unspoken feelings to a genuine sympathy which helps the young person to feel understood – not tolerated, patronized.' The feeling of being understood gives adolescents a sense of safety similar to that which younger children feel when their parents set limits to their behaviour.

Counselling involves the painstaking exploration of pro-blems; there is an attempt to clarify conflicting issues and discover alternative ways of describing them and/or of dealing with them. Counselling helps people to help them-selves. This helping method (like the problem-solving approach, but unlike some of the other methods) emphasizes the 'self-help' element, the need to call on the inner resources of the person who is in difficulties. To this end, the counsellor provides a supportive relationship which enables young people to search for their *own* answers, to rely on their own resources.

Non-directive therapy is based upon the assumption that individuals have within themselves not only the ability to solve their own problems satisfactorily, but also a growth impulse that makes mature behaviour more satisfying than immature behaviour. Here, the basic principles which guide the therapist are as follows: He or she

1 endeavours to develop a warm, friendly relationship with the adolescent;
2 accepts the adolescent exactly as he or she is;
3 establishes a feeling of permissiveness in the relationship so that the individual feels entirely free to express his or her feelings;
4 attempts to be alert to the feelings expressed by the teenager and to reflect those feelings back in such a manner that he or she gains insight into his or her behaviour;
5 maintains a deep respect for the young person's ability to solve his or her own problems if given an opportunity to do so – the responsibility for making choices and for instituting change is the young person's;
6 if possible, does not attempt to hurry therapy along, since it is a gradual process;
7 does not attempt to direct the individual's actions or conversation in any manner: the child leads the way and the therapist follows.

The therapist establishes only those limitations to the person's behaviour that are necessary to anchor the therapy to the world of reality and to make the child aware of his or her responsibility in the relationship.

Family therapy

There is no space to describe in detail the approach called 'family therapy'. However, family therapy is not so much a school or system of therapy as a basic redefinition of the therapeutic task itself. The target for assessment and intervention is far broader than the youngster. Family therapists attempt to conceptualize the problem in a more horizontal (rather than historical) manner, viewing the client (for our

'We've decided to stay together for your sake.'
Reproduced by permission of *Punch*

purposes, the adolescent) as part of a complex network of personal and family relationships, any aspect of which may have a bearing on the present predicament and, indeed, provide the clue to the 'real' problem. These are often formulated in terms of unsatisfactory patterns of dominance, unclear roles and boundaries for members, poor communication and ineffective decision-making. One of the foremost practitioners of family therapy, Salvador Minuchin, writes in his 1981 book:

Family members do not ordinarily experience themselves as part of this family structure. Every human
being sees herself as a unit, a whole, interacting with
other units. She knows that she affects other individuals'
behaviour, and that they affect hers. And as she interacts
within her family, she experiences the family's mapping
of the world. She knows that some territories are
marked, 'Do as you please'. Others are marked,
'Proceed with caution'. Still others are marked 'Stop'. If
she crosses this limit, the family member will encounter
some regulatory mechanism. At times she will acquiesce;
at other times she will challenge. There are also areas
marked, 'Entrance forbidden'. The consequences of
transgression in these areas carry the strongest affective
components: guilt, anxiety, even banishment and
damnation.

Family therapists see the total network of family trans-
actions as greater than the sum of its parts, hence their
rejection of the parents' labelling of a problem as 'my son's/
daughter's problem' as simplistic.

The family is not a static entity; it changes continuously.
And as children grow into adolescents they bring new
elements into the family system. The peer group gains more
influence. The youngster learns that his or her friends'
families work by different standards and rules. The teenage
culture introduces its values with regard to drugs, sex,
religion, politics and the future. Parents, too, are changing in
ways that I described in chapter 3.

Minuchin observes that the family organism, like the
individual person, moves between two poles: one representing
the security of the known, the other being the exploration
necessary for adaptation to changing conditions. When the
family comes to treatment, it is in difficulty because it is
stuck, trying to maintain old ways which no longer meet the
needs of a changed and changing set of circumstances. The
therapist takes a family (according to Minuchin) 'along the
developmental spiral and creates a crisis that will push the
family in the direction of their own evolution'.

The techniques for creating this crisis or 'creative turmoil' and for putting the family on to a new and harmonious path are many and varied. The issue of the effectiveness of this popular approach still awaits a definitive judgement.

Behaviour modification at home and school

Behaviour modification in the natural environment (see chapter 10) is not only about changing the undersirable behaviour of 'problem children' and adolescents, but also about altering the behaviour of the people (parents, teachers and others) who form a significant part of the child's social world. Help is directed to the modification of that environment rather than withdrawing the child from it. The parents (or teachers) become the real agents of change in a very active partnership with the psychologist, thus contributing to the problem of extending positive changes over time.

The most useful and practical way of looking at home and school problems is to see them as located in the relationships between individuals (or between persons and social systems) rather than solely lying within the personalities of the individuals concerned. Most children and teenagers presenting problems in the classroom can be dealt with in a normal school environment, even when the root cause of the problem lies outside purely school factors (e.g. parental relationships). Even in situations of extreme difficulty there are constructive actions which can be taken which may avoid the necessity to exclude problematic adolescents. This, of course, presupposes that the school is receptive to alternative approaches.

In the case of teenagers whose behaviour is particularly aggressive or challenging, clinical or educational psychologists and social workers are not likely to be able to provide immediate solutions. Rather, their role is to be able to promote coping strategies which provide an environment where solutions are more likely to evolve. They provide parents with the skills to manage their children's problem behaviour, which is the subject of the next chapter.

Chapter Ten

Ways of changing problem behaviour

Understanding the problem

The nature of transitions, discussed in chapter 3, provides the *context* in which adolescent problems can be more readily understood. It takes into account *past events* (the individual's 'history') and the painfulness of putting familiar, comfortable old ways behind one. But the here-and-now is also critically important for getting to grips with whatever it is that is troubling your son or daughter.

When problems are deeply rooted and intractable, a careful analysis or assessment of current events and circumstances becomes essential if change is to be initiated. The questions 'what', 'why' and 'how' must be asked in order to *describe* what form the problems take (in all their complexity); to *explain* why they have come about and persist (despite all efforts to modify them); and to work out how to *intervene* so as to bring about a reduction or elimination of the difficulties.

It is important to be precise when describing a problem. Do not describe the adolescent in terms of what you think he or she is ('He's aggressive') or has ('She has a lot of insecurity in her'). Describe the boy or girl in terms of observables — what they do and/or say ('She frequently hits out at her sister and younger brother when she can't get her own way'; 'He more often than not refuses to comply when I ask him to do something or to stop doing something').

Some parents dwell on the past when they look for the source of their offspring's difficulties. It is important to maintain a balance between past and present when trying to find reasons or causes for current behaviour. Prolonged and guilt-ridden 'post-mortems' going back to the teenager's earliest years, wondering whether you 'should' have done X or 'should not' have done Y, are not very constructive. You cannot change the past and, in any event, it is only in rare instances that current problems can be traced to specific past experiences with any degree of confidence. What is clear from broadly based surveys is that, despite all the allegedly harmful factors blamed in the literature for this or that problem (be they adverse parental characteristics, family conflicts, etc.), it is possible to identify significant numbers of children subjected to these influences who developed without serious problems.

Certainly we can point to influences that indirectly predispose young people to certain difficulties. They set the stage in the broadest of terms. Those practitioners who are behaviourally orientated will lose little sleep over the doubts and uncertainties about the precursors of adolescent problems – the tenuousness of the link between conditions (home and school circumstances) far removed in time from present manifestations of troublesome behaviour.

Human actions – whether simple or elaborate, normal or abnormal – are brought about by *many* influences rather than a single factor. Whatever the influence of heredity, personality traits, attitudes and ideas, shaped over years of learning and development (the so-called predisposing causes) the adolescent's day-to-day actions are powerfully controlled by current events, such as opportunities and temptations to transgress (inviting, unsupervised shop shelves; open car or house windows), the accessibility of alcohol and drugs, the proximity to would-be 'tempters' (drug users or pushers, truants, dropouts).

Factors that are crucial because of their *direct* influence on behaviour are the circumstances whereby individuals *learn* to behave in acceptable or unacceptable ways, and the events which precede and follow particular actions, making them more or less likely to be *performed*.

Knowledge of these factors allows parents to play a part in shaping events, rather than trailing helplessly after them, and to look optimistically to the present and future, rather than regretfully to the past.

How behaviour is learned

Normally, a person's behaviour is controlled by its immediate results. Actions that have favourable outcomes tend to be repeated; those with painful or unrewarding consequences tend to be extinguished, that is to say, reduced and eliminated. This form of learning is referred to as instrumental or operant conditioning. It provides us with a form of training in which we can increase the frequency of a behaviour (which occurs quite spontaneously in the individual) by following its appearance with a reward (i.e. by reinforcing it). We are *not* necessarily confined to tangible rewards. They may consist of words of praise, approval or encouragement. Here are some rules of thumb:

Acceptable behaviour	+ Reinforcement	= More acceptable behaviour
Acceptable behaviour	+ No reinforcement	= Less acceptable behaviour
Unacceptable behaviour	+ Reinforcement	= More unacceptable behaviour
Unacceptable behaviour	+ No reinforcement	= Less unacceptable behaviour

Parents and teachers may provide faulty or ineffectual direction because of a lack of attention to the details of training, or through inconsistency. The child may not know the rules, what is expected. Some parents and teachers overreact to certain disciplinary situations, thus undermining their effectiveness and eventually their own confidence. A mother or father who feels depressed, hostile or anxious can misjudge a 'confrontation' and make it worse. To help them to remain calm and competent in these circumstances, it is useful to think of this sequence as the ABC of behaviour:

Antecedent events are the detailed interactions and circumstances that *usually* set the stage for, or trigger,

the problem behaviours/confrontations. They make up the events that lead up to those
Behaviours that you are concerned about, which, in turn, lead to predictable
Consequences, interactions (e.g. naggings, arguments, prolonged shouting, giving-in, etc.).

There can be a chain of events (As) leading up to the problem behaviour(s) followed by a chain of events (Cs) – all of which should be analysed in order to understand why distressing confrontations persist. Here are some examples of these chains. They illustrate the way we increase undesirable behaviour. They are taken from a typical day in the life of Justine, aged 13, who was described at home and at school as disobedient and disruptive.

Antecedents	Behaviour	Consequences
1 Justine was told it was time to get dressed for school. (request/instruction)	She said she didn't want to, and wouldn't. (disobedience)	Her father came and tried to reason with her to get up, for ten minutes at least.
2 At school she kept talking to the pupil next to her and was asked to stop. (instruction, following inappropriate behaviour)	She took no notice. (disobedience)	Justine's teacher shouted at her. She shouted back. All the pupils stopped work to watch the episode.
3 Justine came in from school. She walked all over the house, dumping her clothes and equipment on the floor. (inappropriate, untidy behaviour)	She ignored her mother's requests, and then said, 'I won't!' (disobedience)	Her mother pleaded with her to put her things away. Her mother let her get away with it as she was too busy to insist.

Antecedents	Behaviour	Consequences
4 Justine was told to switch off the TV programme because a visitor had come in. (instruction following inappropriate behaviour)	She argued about keeping it on. She swore at her mother. (disobedience/ verbal aggression)	After a lengthy confrontation it was left on to give everyone a bit of peace.
5 She wanted to go to the disco; her father said she wasn't to go because of the delinquent girls and boys who congregate at club. (instruction)	She shouted abuse and went on about how hard done by she was, and how differently her friends were treated by their parents. (confrontation/ abuse/coercion)	Her father gave way; Justine went to the disco and was late back.

The antecedents (As), you will have notices, began often with inappropriate behaviour which necessitated a reprimand or command which in turn led to non-compliant behaviour, followed by a series of inconsequential events or self-defeating outcomes. Such parental mismanagement should be tackled at the antecedent *and* consequent ends of the behavioural equations. Youngsters need to know what appropriate behaviour is expected; commands/requests must be made in an authoritative but polite manner. Outcomes must be predictable and appropriate. In all the above instances (the Cs), Justine's difficult behaviour was in fact rewarded: either she got her own way, or she achieved some other 'pay-off'. In other words, she received positive reinforcement for behaving in an unacceptable way, which made it more likely to occur again.

We know that parents and teachers are particularly potent sources of social rewards (reinforcements) influencing learning, attitudes and values when children are still young; but their influence continues later in the child's development, well into adolescence and beyond, shaping specific activities and behaviours. The adolescent's peers, especially those who are considered prestigious, also constitute an important source of reinforcement and thus affect the young person's actions.

The whole issue of the nature and timing of reinforcement is complex. What we do know is that the time intervening between an action and its reinforcement is very important; the shorter the interval, the more it is strengthened for future occasions.

An individual's behaviour is affected by much more than the particular nature of reinforcements or goals. The effect of reinforcement depends on whether or not the person perceives a causal relationship between the behaviour and the reward. This perception may vary in degree from individual to individual and even within the same individual over time and situations. A truly significant influence on behaviour is provided by the person's anticipation that the goals will be achieved. Such expectations are determined by his or her previous experience.

Parents or teachers can use the ABC method to 'unravel' a complex or seemingly obscure situation. It could help them understand why a young person's undesirable behaviour is persisting, despite all disciplinary efforts.

Let us take the example of Peter, who is disruptive during Miss Smith's English classes. Peter is not very good at English, since his ability to read is well below that expected for his chronological age. Miss Smith is young and inexperienced, and feels she cannot let Peter 'get away with being cheeky and provocative', but she does not know how to deal with his disruptiveness without making matters worse. When she referred to Peter as an 'undisciplined brat', a 'rather nasty piece of work', 'disruptive' and 'disorderly', Mrs Simpson, the art teacher, and Mr Jackson, the mathematics teacher, were surprised to hear these critical comments, since they seemed to be describing someone quite different from the Peter they knew.

It is important to note that in the ABC analysis (see figure 8)

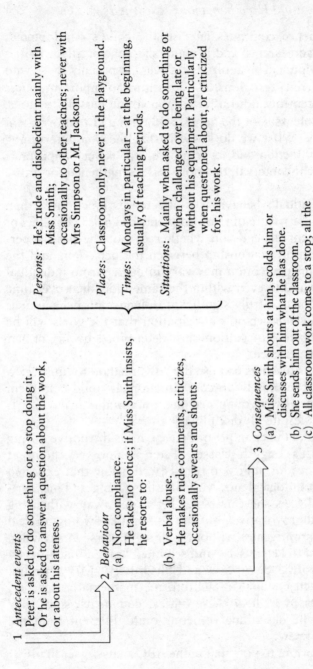

1 *Antecedent events*
Peter is asked to do something or to stop doing it.
Or he is asked to answer a question about the work, or about his lateness.

2 *Behaviour*
(a) Non compliance.
He takes no notice; if Miss Smith insists, he resorts to:

(b) Verbal abuse.
He makes rude comments, criticizes, occasionally swears and shouts.

Persons: He's rude and disobedient mainly with Miss Smith; occasionally to other teachers; never with Mrs Simpson or Mr Jackson.

Places: Classroom only, never in the playground.

Times: Mondays in particular – at the beginning, usually, of teaching periods.

Situations: Mainly when asked to do something or when challenged over being late or without his equipment. Particularly when questioned about, or criticized for, his work.

3 *Consequences*
(a) Miss Smith shouts at him, scolds him or discusses with him what he has done.
(b) She sends him out of the classroom.
(c) All classroom work comes to a stop; all the pupils watch the confrontation.
(d) The original cause of the confrontation is forgotten.

Figure 8 ABC analysis of disruptive behaviour in school

Peter is not disruptive in Mrs Simpson's and Mr Jackson's classes. Mrs Simpson is a young teacher (so it does not seem to be inexperience, youth or gender that encourage Peter's rudeness). She has a sense of humour and uses it to defuse fraught situations. An enquiry about Peter's art work would indicate that it is rather promising, and Peter gets his fair share of praise for his efforts. In fact, one of his pictures was hung up in the place of honour once, for being the best work of the week. Peter is poor at maths – Mr Jackson's subject – but Mr Jackson is quietly encouraging and helpful. His 'stern' voice, in contrast to his generally mild manner, is usually sufficient to quell any incipient disruption – not that it happens very frequently.

To change this unacceptable situation, Miss Smith will need to take a hard look at her relationship with Peter, Peter's difficulties in doing her subject and the chip on his shoulder because of what looks like his low self-esteem. It is not only that the consequences of these confrontations (and of his misbehaviour) are rewarding to him, but there also follows a distraction from the hated lesson. More important are the questions: Why does he need to behave in this way? What problem is he trying to solve by behaving in this manner? Is he capable of earning her attention, peer approval and other reinforcers by showing more acceptable behaviour?

How to improve young people's behaviour

It is reassuring to realize that what has been learned can be unlearned; that young people (like anyone else) can unlearn self-defeating behaviours; that they can learn new, more advantageous ways of going about things; and that parents and teachers are generally the best persons to help them achieve the necessary changes. This means that *you* can learn new ways of managing situations.

Many of the problems that face parents and teachers in the management of adolescents can be handled by using procedures designed to increase the occurance of already existing behaviours.

Positive reinforcement. In order to improve or increase your teenager's performance of certain actions, arrange matters so that an immediate reward follows the correct performance of the desired behaviour. You might indicate your intentions by saying, for example, '*When* you have done your homework, *then* you can go out.' The 'when ... then' formula reminds you that you only reward after the desired action is carried out.

Once an action is well established in an individual's repertoire, the chances are that the behaviour will stay improved if the amount of reinforcement is reduced. This is accomplished by switching over from what is called continuous reinforcement to intermittent reinforcement. The achievement of such a transition prevents the individual from becoming satiated by reward. Words of praise and encouragement offered every so often, at such a stage, can be very reinforcing.

Developing new behaviour patterns. Secure teenagers' co-operation by guiding and helping them towards some desirable action or way of thought. Use a combination of suggestion, appreciation of their difficulties, praise for their efforts and pleasure at their success. Imagination, stimulation and encouragement are all part of the caring parents' strategies when wishing to get the best out of their children.

Shaping (successive approximations). In order to encourage adolescents to act in ways in which they have seldom or never before behaved, reward any action that approximates the behaviour you want. While guiding them through mini-steps towards a goal, you continue to reinforce the approximations to the behaviour you wish to elicit. No reinforcement is given to 'wrong' behaviours. Gradually you make the criteria more and more stringent until, finally, they are only rewarded for the precise behavioural sequence that is required.

'Artificial' versus 'natural' incentives. Incentives are considered artificial if the 'rewards' would not normally occur as

a consequence of the behaviour outside the training or treatment situation (e.g. being given points for, say, being punctual). They are considered 'natural' if the 'rewards' used to strengthen the behaviour during training or treatment closely resemble those normally resulting from that behaviour outside the training situation (e.g. being complimented for being well dressed). Therefore 'natural' as opposed to 'artificial' incentives would normally result in more permanent training effects.

Modelling. In order to teach young people a new pattern of behaviour, give them the opportunity to observe a person who is important to them performing the desired behaviour.

Skills training. Simulate real-life situations in which skills are to be developed. These have been described in chapter 9.

Stopping inappropriate behaviour (extinction). To get young people to desist from acting in a particular way, try to arrange conditions so that they receive no rewards after the undesired acts. Ignore (in other words, pretend not to notice) minor misdemeanours such as sulking and pestering or cheeking. What is called *extinction* can be a very effective procedure for reducing undesirable school-related behaviours. Used by itself or in combination with other procedures, it has demonstrated its effectiveness in a wide variety of situations.

Though the behavioural reduction achieved by means of extinction may take time to accomplish, the effect can be longlasting. Efficient use of extinction requires the removal of *all* reinforcing consequences for the undesirable behaviour. The process can be speeded up if desirable behaviours are reinforced simultaneously with the extinction of undesirable behaviours.

Withhold reinforcements such as approval, attention, and the like, which have previously and inappropriately followed inappropriate behaviour. Remember: *your teenager may 'work hard' to regain the lost reinforcement and thus may get 'worse' before he or she gets 'better'.* If the problem behaviour has been continuously reinforced in the past, then extinction should be relatively swift, since it is much easier for the youngster to recognize that he or she has lost reinforcers than it is for the person receiving intermittent reinforcement. In the latter case, extinction tends to be slow.

Time-out. 'Time-out from positive reinforcement' is a method that has frequently demonstrated its effectiveness in reducing undesirable behaviour. In this approach, the opportunity to obtain reinforcement contingent upon the undesirable behaviour is completely and consistently removed. If the opportunity to earn reinforcement for alternative desirable behaviours is provided at other times, time-out can achieve its goal quite effectively. Used by itself, however, time-out is neither positive nor constructive. For example, if an under-achieving youngster with low self-esteem can only obtain his teacher's attention and his peers' approval by behaving badly, time-out will be ineffective unless it is combined with attention for things he *can* do well. These may have to be sought.

Time-out is a familiar procedure to the teacher; it has probably been used by most teachers at one time or another. Teachers have long used the procedure of placing a child outside the room, or at the back of a room, or excluding him or her from an activity (say, a game). There is disagreement about how far it is effective in changing classroom behaviour. It does have the advantage of providing both the teacher and the pupil with a breathing space in which tempers can cool, thus avoiding the use of harsher methods of control. Time-out has a number of counter-productive effects for the disruptive pupil. He or she is in the limelight, possibly acting the buffoon and therefore still the centre of attention. Or the pupil is getting out of doing some unwelcome scholastic task, or getting away from a sarcastic teacher. If this is the case, the teacher should take a hard look at his or her teaching and/or interactions with this individual.

A critical determinant of the effectiveness of time-out is the extent to which the adolescent actually enjoys the situation from which he or she is removed. If that situation is positively frightening, anxiety-provoking or boring, it is possible that the time-out procedure might involve removing the youngster to a less aversive situation and thereby actually *increase*, rather than decrease, the frequency of the inappropriate behaviour. It will have had rewarding rather than punishing outcomes.

Overcorrection (restitutional overcorrection). Here one requires individuals to correct the consequences of their misbehaviour. They must not only remedy the situation they have caused but also 'overcorrect' it, so that the situation is improved to better than normal. In other words, one enforces the performance of a new behaviour in the situation where it is required to become routine.

Overcorrection (positive practice). Here the youngster is made to practise positive behaviours which are physically incompatible with the inappropriate behaviour. For instance, a girl who steals and breaks another girl's bracelet is required to save up enough money not only to replace the object but also to buy a small gift betokening regret. She is praised at the completion of the act of restitution. A boy who deliberately punctures another child's bicycle tyre not only has to repair the tyre but also must oil and polish the entire vehicle.

Response cost. To stop your teenager from acting in a particular way, arrange for him or her to pre-empt or terminate a *mildly* unpleasant situation by changing his or her behaviour in the desired direction. For example, the television is turned off for a minute every time the youngster offers an obscenity-laden commentary on what is happening.

Relaxation. The following exercises are suggested by clinical psychologist Reg Beech (1985). Most people require about three weeks of daily practice in order to achieve a useful level of skill at relaxing at will. The exercises all involve the following general steps:

1 Lightly tense a given group of muscles (as listed below) and hold this tension for a slow count of 5 while holding your breath.
2 During (1) above, focus your attention on the sensations in the part of your body that has been brought under tension.
3 At the end of 5 seconds, breathe out, relax the tense muscles *as much as possible*, focusing your mind on the new relaxed sensations in that part of your body.
4 While letting go (as in (3) above), think of the words 'calm yourself' and 'relax'.
5 Allow your muscles to relax completely and, in your mind, compare the feelings of tension just experienced with the relaxation you now feel.

The particular exercises are as follows:

Arms. Clench the fists and tighten the muscles of both arms, holding your arms stiff and straight out in front of you.
Legs. Raise both legs (or one, if preferred) about 12–18 inches from their resting position, point the toes and stiffen the legs so that thigh and calf muscles are brought under tension. Repeat with other leg if necessary.
General torso. Pull the shoulders back, bringing shoulder blades together, push the chest forward and out and, at the same time, use appropriate muscles to *pull in* the stomach, making a hollow in that part of your body.
Neck. Press the head firmly against the support of the chair back or mattress.
Face. There are three separate exercises here:

(a) Raise the eyebrows, forcing them up as far as you can as if trying to make them meet your hair line.
(b) Screw up your eyes tightly and, at the same time, wrinkle your nose and compress lips hard.
(c) Clench the jaws, as if chewing hard, while pushing your tongue hard against the roof of your mouth.

Remember, each of the above exercises is immediately preceded by taking a deep breath, creating tension, and holding it for 5 seconds, then exhaling while letting go the tension and saying the word 'relax' to yourself. In each case try to focus your mind on that part of your body that has been made tense and relaxed, in turn.

Don't try to hurry the programme of exercises, which should take about 20 minutes or so. After each separate exercise allow a minute or so for fuller relaxation to take place and for you to concentrate on the pleasant sensations that relaxation brings.

Cognitive control. What people say to themselves, and how they interpret situations, influences their behaviour; faulty thinking can lead to 'faulty' actions, and may be revealed in what children tell themselves ('self-talk'). So changing their self-talk, and (hopefully) their cognitions, may benefit the way they act and feel.

1 *Correcting self-talk.* Self-talk is a major preoccupation of all of us when we are beset with trials and tribulations. 'I can't cope any more . . . I'm in a terrible mess.'

To help adolescents (and, indeed, parents at times) we examine and dissect some of the faulty reasoning underlying the self-talk: the exaggerations ('No one loves me', 'There's *no* hope!'), the need to be all-competent, to show no weakness, to be acknowledged and loved *all* the time, to be for ever right. Counselling on such illogicalities, the prompting and practising of new self-talk ('I can manage . . . I'm a good mother'; 'Think first, act afterwards . . . Keep cool'), may bring some relief.

2 *Modifying interpretations and awareness.* Modifying a youngster's cognitions concerning an unpleasant experience might reduce its probability of triggering violent behaviour. To take an example, if the incident of another person knocking over the potential aggressor is *redefined* as an accident rather than an attack, there may be less risk of a pugnacious reaction.

The influence of pleasant or aversive consequences on a person's actions are enhanced by his or her awareness of these consequences. Thus increasing consciousness of the penalties contingent upon aggressive behaviour may reduce its performance.

3 *Using stress – management strategies.* There is evidence that the performance of (say) aggressive acts can be influenced by

(a) being able to recognize problematic situations when they occur (preparing for provocation);
(b) making an attempt to resist the temptation to act impulsively or to do nothing to deal with the situation (controlling the reaction to the confrontation);
(c) defining the situation in concrete terms and formulating the major issues to be coped with; deciding on the course(s) of action most likely to result in positive consequences (coping with arousal);
(d) finally, verifying the effectiveness of the coping procedures in resolving the problematic situation (reflecting on the experience).

A number of procedures are available for the purposes of controlling impulsive actions; they include self-recording by the child of hostile activities, together with his or her observations of the circumstances in which they occurred and their consequences.

A psychologist R. W. Novaco provides the client with positive self-statements for dealing with anger:

Preparing for Provocation

This is going to upset me, but I know how to deal with it.

What is it that I have to do?

I can work out a plan to handle this.

I can manage the situation. I know how to regulate my anger.

If I find myself getting upset, I'll know what to do.

There won't be any need for an argument.

Try not to take this too seriously.

This could be a testy situation, but I believe in myself.

Time for a few deep breaths of relaxation. Feel

comfortable, relaxed, and at ease.
Easy does it. Remember to keep your sense of humour.

Reacting during the Confrontation

Stay calm. Just continue to relax.
As long as I keep my cool, I'm in control.
Just roll with the punches; don't get bent out of shape.
Think of what you want to get out of this.
You don't need to prove yourself.
There is no point in getting mad.
Don't make more out of this than you have to.
I'm not going to let him get to me.
Look for the positives. Don't assume the worst or jump to conclusions.
It's really a shame that she has to act like this.
For someone to be that irritable, he must be awfully unhappy.
If I start to get mad, I'll just be banging my head against the wall. So I might as well just relax.
There is no need to doubt myself. What he says doesn't matter.
I'm on top of this situation and it's under control.

Coping with Arousal

My muscles are starting to feel tight. Time to relax and slow things down.
Getting upset won't help.
It's just not worth it to get so angry.
I'll let him make a fool of himself.
I have a right to be annoyed, but let's keep the lid on.
Time to take a deep breath.
Let's take the issue point by point.
My anger is a signal of what I need to do. Time to instruct myself.
I'm not going to get pushed around, but I'm not going haywire either.
Try to reason it out. Treat each other with respect.
Let's try a cooperative approach. Maybe we are both right.

Negatives lead to more negatives. Work constructively.
He'd probably like me to get really angry. Well I'm
   going to disappoint him.
I can't expect people to act the way I want them to.
Take it easy, don't get pushy.

Reflecting on the Experience

When conflict is unresolved:
   Forget about the aggravation. Thinking about it only
      makes you upset.
   These are difficult situations, and they take time to
      straighten out.
   Try to shake it off. Don't let it interfere with your job.
   I'll get better at this as I get more practice.
   Remember relaxation. It's a lot better than anger.
   Can you laugh about it? It's probably not so serious.
   Don't take it personally.
   Take a deep breath and think positive thoughts.

When conflict is resolved or coping is successful:
   I handled that one pretty well. It worked!
   That wasn't as hard as I thought.
   It could have been a lot worse.
   I could have become more upset than it was worth.
   I actually got through that without getting angry.
   My pride can sure get me into trouble, but when I
      don't take things too seriously, I'm better off.
   I guess I've been getting upset for too long when it
      wasn't even necessary.
   I'm doing better at this all the time.

Agreements and contracts

It may seem odd or demeaning to negotiate an agreement –
perhaps even draw up a written contract – with a son or
daughter. Yet such procedures can be extremely effective in
easing interpersonal difficulties and disagreements. Problems
are seldom unilateral: it takes two or more to quarrel or
disagree.

It may seem crass and commercial, but there *is* an element of exchange and bargaining in the conduct of many of our personal relationships. Social interactions and relationships can be compared figuratively to economic bargains or the exchange of gifts: they are seen as a ratio of rewards and costs. All activities carried out by one individual, to the benefit of another, are termed 'rewards', while detrimental activities – hostility, anxiety, embarrassment – are counted as 'costs'. If a teenager forgoes a reward (e.g. loses the approval of his or her family) because he or she engages in some form of social interaction (e.g. associating with a delinquent), this too is termed a cost. The ratio of rewards to costs is called the 'outcome': if the outcome is positive, it may be said to yield a 'profit'; if negative, it is termed a 'loss'.

Relationships break down when the 'debit' column over a long period heavily outweighs the 'credit' column, resulting in a state of chronic loss. Many marriages end like this, and countless friendships founder.

Contracts can be used to restore a profit in mutual relationships. Agreements (whether written down or agreed verbally) have the effect of structuring reciprocal exchanges. They specify who is to do what, for whom, and under what circumstances. Reinforcements (to take one example) can be made explicit between individuals who wish to bring about behaviour change (e.g. parents, teachers), and those whose behaviour is to be changed (students, teenagers). Reciprocal contractual agreements are not unnatural to most people; they exist in families and other groupings, whether explicit or implicit.

In some family exchanges there is, sadly, very little co-operation, not much in the way of kindly, mutually rewarding actions or words. Rather there is an excess of mutual criticism, recrimination and threat. ('If you do X, I will pay you back with Y', or 'Until you listen and do Z, I will continue to do Y'.) The harmony and 'give and take' of affectionate, thoughtful family life have been put to flight. In such circumstances it is usually more fruitful to attend to *family* relationships themselves, rather than with the resentful parents alone, or with only the teenager who is allegedly 'at odds' with everyone.

Contracts are potentially valuable because they necessitate discussion, they encourage communication about personal and family goals, and they involve negotiation, thus teaching the art of compromise. Their function is to provide an agreement about rules of conduct which cannot be changed unilaterally or arbitrarily – that is, without further discussion and agreement. They can include penalties for breaking the terms of the contract, and they can provide the foundation stone for the development of mutual trust. At a time of crisis, when teenagers and their parents (or brothers and sisters) are angry and resentful, contracts provide an opportunity for a family to take stock and to break through vicious circles of retribution and unreason.

The main assumptions underlying the use of *formal* verbal agreements, or the stronger, written form of contract, are as follows. First, a publicly endorsed, unambiguous and specific commitment to a future course of action will prove more binding, a better guarantee of compliance, than more casual 'promises' or ephemeral statements of intention. Secondly, to obtain such results, the parties concerned must not feel they have been unduly coerced into their contractual arrangements. Thirdly, the most potent reinforcers (rewards) available to change the behaviour of the person *causing* the problem reside within the person who is experiencing the *effects* of the problem. Thus a pre-planned and simultaneous alteration in actions from *both* parties, on either side of the problem, is required to achieve a happy outcome.

When making a contract, remember the following points:

1 Be very specific in spelling out the desired actions.
2 Pay attention to the details of the *privileges* and *conditions* both parties to the agreement expect to gain from it. (Parents may want their son to complete his homework and attend school regularly; he, on the other hand, desires more free time with his friends, or more pocket money.)
3 Those actions chosen for the youngster to fulfil must be

readily observable. (If parents or teachers are unable to discern whether an obligation has been met, they cannot grant a privilege.) This requirement applies also to parents.

4 The contract should impose sanctions for a failure to fulfil the agreement. Each party should know precisely what the penalties are for breaking the contract. The sanctions are agreed to *in advance*, are decided by both sides, and are applied *consistently*.

5 There can be no arbitrary, unilateral tinkering with the terms of the contract after the signing. (Changes must be negotiated and agreed to by both sides.)

6 A contract can provide a bonus clause so that extra privileges, special activities, etc., are available to both parties, for consistent performance over a long time.

7 There should be a built-in scheme for monitoring the amount of positive reinforcement given and received. (The records are kept – a chart or notebook – to inform each participant of the progress, or lack of it, of the agreement.)

The practical details of a contract must be carefully thought out. In the case of an informal agreement, which is most applicable where one is dealing with day-to-day conflicts, you should first select behaviours to encourage or change. If you wish your son or daughter to show *more* behaviours of a particular kind, in choosing them remember that they should be (a) important (as opposed to trivial) and (b) functional. If actions with a practical function are manifested more frequently, the youngster will have a better chance of obtaining from his or her environment the *natural* kinds of rewards which most people desire and enjoy, such as praise and esteem. Some contracts about poor relationships emphasize reciprocity and mutual obligations. Others require unilateral change which will be rewarded.

If you wish your youngster to *desist* from certain actions and activities, try to express these in terms of positive change. For example, if you would like your son to stop being cheeky and abusive, specify change as requiring him to address people in a polite and courteous manner. This would then have to be spelled out in terms of specific examples of behaviour.

Before making the agreement, sit down with your teenager and explain the purpose of the exercise – to help make family life more pleasant. Write down five items of behaviour (actions) you wish your son or daughter would do more often. Don't be vague (e.g. 'I wish she'd be more helpful'); be concrete and specific (e.g. 'I wish she'd help me set and clear the table'). For example, vague and unhelpful goals for teenagers are:

Margaret should come in on time.
Elizabeth must improve her personal appearance.
Jeffrey's poor attitude towards his teachers has to change.
Donald's reactions to frustration get him into trouble at
  school.

In the case of a *formal* agreement, write out or type the terms of the contract (a simple example is given below) and have it signed by both parties to the agreement.

Contract

Between Mr and Mrs Smith and Anne Smith.

Mother and father would like Anne to:

1   let them know about her movements when she goes out at night; Anne will let them know about her movements when she goes out at night *by*:
      telling them where she is and with whom;
      letting them know when she'll be home.

2   be less moody; she won't go silent ('sulk') for hours on end when reprimanded or thwarted.

3   be more ready to say sorry; i.e. she will apologize when she's been in the wrong.

4   show more concern about her school work (e.g. homework); i.e. she will put in at least an hour per night.

5   stop being so rude to her father, i.e. walking out when he gives her advice.

Anne would like her mother and father to:

1 stop criticizing her friends all the time; i.e. stop calling them names and saying they're no good, unless they are making a particular, constructive comment.

2 admit when they are in the wrong, i.e. they will apologize when they have been in the wrong in their confrontations with her.

3 give her more pocket money (a sum agreed) and to review the amount every six months in the light of the rising expense and changing nature of her commitments.

All agree

1 that the terms of the contract will not be changed except by mutual discussion and agreement.

2 that disputes will be settled by the witness (grandmother), whom all accept to be objective and fair-minded.

3 that successful execution of the contract for a month will be rewarded by a family treat (first month: an outing to a posh (named) restaurant).

4 that failure to carry out individual terms of the contract will result in a fine on each occasion: an amount of X for Anne; and Y amount for Mr and Mrs Smith respectively. The money is go to in a 'penalty box' (kept by the grandmother), the proceeds of which will go to a charity of her choice.

> *Signed* Anne ....
> Mr Smith ....
> Mrs Smith ....
> Grandmother (witness) ....

Epilogue

It would be quite reasonable to assume that, since adolescence represents the final phase of childhood and the brink of adulthood, parents' memories might be expected to be less dim than they are for other periods. Yet, only too often, we have to admit in anguish or angry resentment, 'I simply cannot understand my child at all.' But when we say 'cannot' do we really mean 'will not'? For some of us, adolescence was none too happy a time. We were relieved to get through it, put it behind us and (except, perhaps, for a few nostalgic events) forget all about it. And within this amnesia not a few deep longings, unresolved fantasies, unrealized ideals and dashed hopes are buried away. But children grow up and suddenly they are at a stage of life which reminds us of it all over again.

In a sense the adolescent in the child awakens the adolescent in the parent – the part that never quite grew up but had to be suppressed by the many compromises adult life requires of people. It is like staring into a mirror when we look closely at the adolescent child; and the image of one's self is, at times, threatened.

For other parents, this interpretation does not apply. Their reasonably benign memories of their teenage years are submerged under the relentless propaganda about the miseries of adolescence and the failings of modern youth. Like the first category of parents, this group is primed to get agitated and to overreact to situations. Their erstwhile biddable child is now unrecognizable – a veritable cuckoo in the nest. Small crises become major problems and there is much sound and fury. It is sad when we try not to remember, not to understand. Because the best thing we can do – even in the face of abuse for our efforts – is to make up for the adolescent's confusion and incomprehension by doing their understanding for them.

I have tried to convey the desirability of keeping a sense of proportion. There is so much to enjoy in the close company of teenagers – their verve, their sense of anticipation and their fresh vision of life. Yes, of course, there are very real problems. But you can survive these by providing a rock-solid base while the adolescent discovers his or her adult status, letting the occasional waves of discontent, criticism and rebellion break around you – without breaking you. This is not to suggest that you remain passively understanding or fatalistically tolerant. Contrary to widely held myths about adolescence, teenagers *are* susceptible – despite their famous reticence and 'prickliness' – to the right sort of help, sensitively proffered. Their minds, at this stage of development, are probably as open as they ever will be. The awkward question may be: 'Is yours?'

I would like to end this book with the words of an adolescent girl. For me they sum up the best of the teenage years: the idealism, the optimism and the courage.

I think change doesn't need to be a bad thing, and I don't think you should be so frightened. There's a lot of things wrong in this world that need changing, and if people are frightened of change, it means they'll probably change for the worst and not the best. I think we should stick together and believe what we believe in, and try and make things better.

Sources of professional help in the UK

The clinic

The traditional treatment of problem behaviour takes place in a clinic or a hospital. Parents bring the child to the professional (a psychiatrist, psychologist or social worker) who works primarily with the child as the client with 'target' problems to be modified. The setting for the therapy is the consulting room and the expert 'treats' the young person. Although the parents and teachers are sometimes advised to be (say) more consistent, warm, loving or understanding, they are often left to their own devices to translate such instructions into action. As a result, many do not know specifically how they should change their handling of the teenager.

Psychologists and psychiatrists

Very often people ask, 'What is the difference between a psychiatrist and a clinical psychologist?' The essential differences are those of training and orientation. Psychiatrists have completed a medical degree and then gone on to specialize in the study and treatment of mental illnesses. Clinical psychologists have taken a degree in academic psychology in a university department before continuing their training in hospitals and postgraduate university courses leading to a professional diploma or degree in clinical psychology.

Clinical psychologists are, then, non-medical specialists in mental-health-related aspects of human nature; but, because human nature, the mind and body cannot be rigidly compartmentalized, much of their training, knowledge and day-to-day work overlaps with that of psychiatrists and other specialists in human problems.

Psychiatrists are qualified doctors who specialize in their field of psychiatry in the same way that other medical people specialize in surgery, obstetrics or paediatrics. They do their internship and residency at a mental hospital or in a teaching hospital for psychiatrists. In most child psychiatric clinics and child guidance clinics, the psychiatrist is one of a team which co-operates on diagnosis and on the planning of a therapeutic programme for the patient. The team (depending on its setting) may include a psychiatrist, clinical psychologist or educational psychologist (in the case of child guidance clinics), psychiatric nurses, a speech therapist, an occupational therapist and a social worker.

Psychiatric social workers

Psychiatric social workers hold a qualification in general social work. Experience and specialist training have been gained in child guidance clinics and psychiatric hospitals. They apply their knowledge of the social sciences to the problems of the adult or child with emotional problems – problems which inevitably have social repercussions and, very probably, social causes. As part of the team approach, the psychiatric social worker will make home visits, and sometimes school visits, and will interview people important in the adolescent's social environment. Apart from collecting information, he or she will give advice and counselling in the hope of modifying attitudes that contribute to the family's problems. Social workers might be involved in sorting out practical social problems. They may contact agencies for the care of children and young adolescents who are without their parents; organize financial and other support for (say) a single parent looking after young children; and arrange for social skills training or a youth club for a teenage client.

Probation officers

Probation officers in Britain receive a generic social work training but specialize in court-related work. Their work brings them into contact with juvenile and young adult offenders and their families. They prepare social enquiry reports for the courts and carry out preventive, supervisory and treatment-orientated casework and community work.

In-patient care

The main focus of this book has been on helping or 'treating' adolescents in their own homes or schools. Day hospital care or in-patient treatment may be required for some of the more serious psychological disorders. Schizophrenia is a mental illness which sometimes has its onset in late adolescence. It is notable for its auditory hallucinations (e.g. voices), disorders of thinking and feeling, and social withdrawal. Professor Rutter lists the reasons for admitting children and teenagers to hospital: disorders that are too severe to be managed outside hospital; the need for relief for the parents when family stress has become too great; the necessity for special treatment methods only available in hospital; the need for a specialized and controlled group-living experience to deal with difficulties in social relationships; the presence of an associated medical condition requiring in-patient treatment; the need for prolonged observation or special tests to assist diagnosis.

The School Psychological Service

In the United Kingdom, the School Psychological Service – which is often linked with child and family guidance centres – aims primarily to offer professional support that will promote the social, emotional and intellectual development and educational progress of children in school and elsewhere and help to ensure that they receive learning opportunities appropriate to their individual needs. An adolescent's problems arise from the interaction of a particular personality and his or her setting – home, school and community. In helping to resolve these problems, educational psychologists in the service draw on insights from social and community psychology and skills in consultation and psychological intervention. A knowledge of child and adolescent development, together with assessment skills, is of central importance and forms the clinical foundation on which a broader contribution is based.

Other sources of help

Special day and residential schools play an important part in helping adolescents with psychological problems which affect their ability to learn and/or adapt to mainstream school life. In addition, a wide range of voluntary and offical facilities contribute to the care, treatment and rehabilitation of young people: local-authority social services, foster care, children's homes, special classes, hostels, holiday camps, addiction units, homes for unmarried young mothers, 'drop-in' centres, counselling centres, and a host of advisory services. Consult your local Citizens' Advice Bureau, social services or probation service for information.

Authors and studies cited

Argyl, M. and Trower, P. (1979) *Person to Person*. London: Harper & Row.

Bandura, A. and Walters, R. H. (1959) *Adolescent Aggression*. New York: Ronald Press.

Baumrind, D. (1975) 'Early socialization and adolescent competence'. In S. E. Dragastin and G. H. Elder (eds), *Adolescence in the Life Cycle*. London: Halsted Press.

Becker, N. C. et al. (1967) 'The contingent use of teacher attention and praise in reducing classroom behaviour problems'. *Journal of Special Education*, 1, 287–307.

Beech, R. (1985) *Staying Together*. Chichester: Wiley.

Belson, W. A. (1975) *Juvenile Theft*. London: Harper & Row.

Clarke, R. V. G. (ed.) (1978) *Tackling Vandalism*. Home Office Research Study, no. 47. London: HMSO.

Coleman, J. C. (1974) *Relationships in Adolescence*. London: Routledge & Kegan Paul.

Conger, J. J. (1973) *Adolescence and Youth*. London: Harper & Row.

Coopersmith, S. (1967) *The Antecedents of Self-Esteem*. London: W. H. Freeman.

De Risi, W. J. and Butz, G. (1975) *Writing Behavioural Contracts*. Champaign, Ill.: Research Press.

Docking, J. W. (1985) 'Classroom control strategies and educational outcomes'. *Maladjustment and Therapeutic Education*, 3, 1, 5–12.

Dominion, J. (1968) *Marital Breakdown*. Harmondsworth: Penguin.

Donovan, A. et al. (1985) 'Employment status and Psychological well-being'. *Journal of Child Psychology and Psychiatry*, 27, 65–76.

Douglas, J. W. B. et al. (1968) *All Our Future*. London: Peter Davies.

Egan, G. (1986) *The Skilled Helper*. Monterey: Brooks/Cole.

Elkind, D. (1980) 'Strategic interactions in early adolescence'. In J. Adelson (ed.), *Handbook of Adolescent Psychology*. New York: Wiley.

Erikson, E. H. (1965) *Childhood and Society*. London: Chatto and Windus: The Hogarth Press.

Erikson, E. H. (1968) *Youth, Identity and Crisis*. New York: Norton.

Ginott, H. (1969) *Between Parent and Child*. London: Staples Press.

Glueck, S. and Glueck, E. T. (1968) *Delinquents and Non-Delinquents in Perspective*. New Haven, Conn.: Harvard University Press.

Hargreaves, D. H. et al. (1975) *Deviance in Classrooms*. London: Routledge & Kegan Paul.

Harris, M. (1969) *Your Teenager*. Corgi Mini-Book. London: Transworld Publishers.

Herbert, M. (1981) *Behavioural Treatment of Problem Children: a practice manual*. London: Academic Press. (2nd edn, revised and updated, 1987).

Herbert, M. (1985) *Caring for your Children: a practical guide*. Oxford: Basil Blackwell.

Herbert, M. (1987) *Conduct Disorders of Childhood and Adolescence*. Chichester: Wiley.

Hersov, L. (1977) 'School refusal'. In M. Rutter and L. Hersov (eds), *Child Psychiatry: modern approaches*. Oxford: Blackwell Scientific.

Holland, J. L. (1973) *Making Vocational Choices*. Englewood Cliffs: Prentice-Hall.

Hopson, B. (1986) 'Transition, understanding and managing personal change'. In M. Herbert (ed.), *Psychology for Social Workers*. London: Macmillan/British Psychological Society.

Institute for the Study of Drug Dependence (1982) *Drug Abuse Briefing*. London: ISDD.

Josselson, R. (1980) 'Ego development in adolescence'. In J. Adelson (ed.), *Handbook of Adolescent Psychology*. New York: Wiley.

Kagan, J. and Moss, H. A. (1962) *Birth to Maturity*. New York: Wiley.

Kuder, F. (1966) *Kuder Occupational Interest Survey: general manual*. Chicago: Science Research Associates.

Lange, H. J. and Jakubowski, P. (1977) *Responsible Assertive Behaviour*. Champaign, Ill.: Research Press.

Lancashire Education Authority (1979) *Active Tutorial Work*, book 2. Oxford: Blackwell.

McClelland, D. (1961) *The Achieving Society*. Princeton, NJ: Van Nostrand.

March, P. and Smith, M. (1977) *Your Choice at 17+*. Cambridge: Hobson's Press.

Meichenbaum, D. H. (1974) *Cognitive Behaviour Modification*. New York: Plenum.

Minuchin, S. and Fishman, H. C. (1981) *Family Therapy Techniques*. London: Harvard University Press.

Morgan, P. (1978) *Juvenile Delinquency: fact and fiction*. London: Temple Smith.

Mothner, I. and Weitz, A. (1986) *How to Get Off Drugs*. Harmondsworth: Penguin.

Nicol, A. R. (1985) *Longitudinal Studies in Child Psychology and Psychiatry*. Chichester: Wiley.

Novaco, R. W. (1975) *Anger Control*. Lexington: Heath.

Open University Course Organizers (1982) *Parents and Teenagers*. London: Harper & Row. Figures 5 and 6 in my book both appear in this excellent course guide.

Palmer, R. (1980) *Anorexia Nervosa*. Harmondsworth: Penguin.

Paranjpe, A. C. (1976) *In Search of Identity*. New York: Wiley.

Parkes, C. M. (1972) *Bereavement*. London: Tavistock.

Patterson, G. R. (1971) *Families: application of social learning to family life*. Champaign, Ill.: Research Press.

Patterson, G. R. (1982) *Coercive Family Process*. Eugene, Oreg.: Castalia.

Phares, E. J. (1976) *Locus of Control in Personality*. Morristown, NJ: General Learning Press.

Power, M. J. et al. (1967) 'Delinquent schools'. *New Society*, 10, 542–3.

Rapoport, R., Rapoport, R. N. and Strelitz, Z. (1977) *Fathers, Mothers and Others*. London: Routledge & Kegan Paul.

Remmers, H. H. and Radler, D. H. (1957) *The American Teenager*. Indianapolis, Ind.: Bobbs-Merrill.

Robins, L. (1966) *Deviant Children Grown Up*. Baltimore, Md: Williams & Wilkins.

Rogers, C. R. (1961) 'The characteristics of helping relationships'. In M. J. Stein (ed.), *Contemporary Psychotherapies*. New York: Free Press.

Rosenthal, R. and Jacobsen, L. (1968) *Pygmalion in the Classroom.* New York: Holt, Rinehart & Winston.

Rutter, M. (1971) 'Normal psychosexual development'. *Journal of Child Psychology and Psychiatry,* 11, 259–83.

Rutter, M. (1979) *Changing Youth in a Changing Society.* London: The Nuffield Provincial Hospitals Trust.

Rutter, M. et al. (1979) *Fifteen Thousand Hours.* London: Open Books.

Schofield, M. (1965) *The Sexual Behaviour of Young People.* London: Longmans Green.

Schofield, M. (1973) *The Sexual Behaviour of Young Adults: a follow-up study.* London: Allen Lane.

Seligman, M. E. P. (1975) *Helplessness: on depression, development and death.* San Francisco: Freeman.

Sorenson, R. C. (1973) *Adolescent Sexuality in Contemporary America.* New York: World Publishing.

Stone, L. J. and Church, J. (1968) *Childhood and Adolescence.* New York: Random House.

Sullivan, H. S. (1953) *The Interpersonal Theory of Psychiatry.* New York: Norton.

Tattum, T. P. (1982) *Disruptive Pupils in Schools and Units.* Chichester: Wiley.

Thompson, O. E. (1971) 'Occupational values of high school students'. In H. D. Thornburg (ed.), *Contemporary Adolescence: readings.* Belmont: Brooks/Cole.

Travers, J. F. (1977) *The Growing Child.* New York: Wiley.

Wellings, K. (1986) *First Love, First Sex: a practical guide to relationships.* Wellingborough: Thorsons.

West, D. (1977) *The Delinquent Way of Life.* London: Heinemann Educational.

West, D. J. and Farrington, D. P. (1973) *Who Becomes Delinquent?* London: Heinemann Educational.

Woods, P. (1984) 'A sociological analysis of disruptive incidents'. In N. Froude and H. Gault (eds), *Disruptive Behaviour in Schools.* Chichester: Wiley.

Wright, D. (1971) *The Psychology of Moral Behaviour.* Harmondsworth: Penguin.

Youniss, J. (1980) *Parents and Peers in Social Development.* Chicago: University of Chicago Press.

Further reading

Chapter One

Coleman, J. (1980) *Nature of Adolescence*. London: Methuen.
Conger, J. (1979) *Adolescence: generation under pressure*. London: Harper & Row.

Chapter Two

Herbert, M. (1985) *Caring for your Children: a practical guide*. Oxford: Basil Blackwell.

Chapter Three

Baldwin, D. (1981) *Know your Body*. Harmondsworth: Penguin.
Irwin, E. (1979) *Growing Pains: a study of teenage distress*. London: MacDonald & Evans.
Laufer, M. (1975) *Adolescent Disturbance and Breakdown*. Harmondsworth: Penguin.
Rubin, M. (1981) *Women of a Certain Age: the midlife search for self*. London: Harper Colophon Books.

Chapter Four

Herbert, M. (1987) *Conduct Disorders of Childhood and Adolescence: a social learning perspective*. Chichester: Wiley.

Chapter Five

Barlow, D. (1981) *Sexually Transmitted Diseases – the Facts*. Oxford: Oxford University Press.
Belfield, T. and Martins, H. (1984) *Introduction to Family Planning*. London: Family Planning Association.

Cahill, M. M. (1984) *The Aids Epidemic.* London: Hutchinson.

Claesson, B. H. (1980) *Boy, Girl, Man, Woman: a guide to sex for young children.* Harmondsworth: Penguin.

Clarity Collective (1986) *Taught not Caught: strategies for sex education.* Wisbech: Learning Development Aids.

Dalton, K. (1978) *Once a Month.* London: Fontana.

Forward, S. and Buck, C. (1981) *Betrayal of Innocence: incest and devastation.* Harmondsworth: Penguin.

Griffin, S. (1981) *Pornography and Silence.* London: The Women's Press.

Hart, J. (1984) *So you Think You Are Attracted to the Same Sex?* Harmondsworth: Penguin.

Hawton, K. (1985) *Sex Therapy: a practical guide.* Oxford: Oxford University Press.

Rudinger, E. (ed.) (1984) *Pregnancy Month by Month.* London: Comsumers' Association.

Went, D. J. (1985) *Sex Education: some guidelines for teachers.* London: Bell & Hyman.

Chapter Six

Careers Information Service (1979) *Careers A–Z.* London: Collins.

Chapter Seven

Miller, P. M. (1976) *Behavioural Treatment of Alcoholism.* Oxford: Pergamon.

Mothner, I. and Weitz, A. (1986) *How to Get Off Drugs.* Harmondsworth: Penguin.

Chapter Eight

David, K. and Cowley, J. (1980) *Pastoral Care in Schools and Colleges.* London: Edward Arnold.

Goldstein, A. P. et al. (1983) *School Violence.* Englewood Cliffs: Prentice-Hall.

Chapter Nine

Duck, S. (1977) *The Study of Acquaintance.* Farborough: Saxon House.

Egan, G. (1977) *You and Me: the skills of communicating and relating to others*. Englewood Cliffs: Prentice-Hall.

Ellis, A. (1974) *Disputing Irrational Beliefs*. New York: Institute for Rational Living.

Gordon, T. (1970) *Parent Effectiveness Training*. New York: Peter H. Wyden.

Nelson-Jones, R. (1986) *Human Relationship Skills: training and self-help*. London: Holt, Rinehart & Winston.

Wilkinson, J. and Canter, S. (198) *Social Skills Training Manual*. Chichester: Wiley.

Chapter Ten

Herbert, M. (1987) *Behavioural Treatment of Problem Children: a practice manual*. London: Academic Press.

Index

Index by Mandy Crook